D0118993

LIVING
LEGACIES

LIVING LEGACIES

How to Write, Illustrate, and Share Your Life Stories

Duane Elgin and Coleen LeDrew

CONARI PRESS

Cover Collage: Sondra Holtzman
Cover Photography: Richard Sargent
Cover Design: Birgit Wick
Interior Design and Composition: Birgit Wick
Interior Collages: Birgit Wick in collaboration with Coleen LeDrew, and with contributions by Gwen Gordon and the other story creators.

Library of Congress Cataloging-in-Publication Data
Elgin, Duane.
   Living legacies : how to write, illustrate, and share your life
stories / Duane Elgin and Coleen LeDrew.
      p. cm.
   Includes bibliographical references.
   ISBN 1-57324-552-6
   1. Autobiography--Authorship. 2. Report writing. I. LeDrew, Coleen.
II. Title.
  CT25 .E44 2000
  808'.06692--dc21
                                        00-011498

Printed in the United States of America
00 01 02 RRD (NW) 10 9 8 7 6 5 4 3 2 1

This book is dedicated

to those who want to leave their legacy,

to our families and friends for sharing their legacies,

to the ancestors who have left their legacies,

to future generations who will inherit our legacy.

This book is also dedicated

to Elaine and Fred LeDrew

for their faith, support, and encouragement.

Contents

Contents

Contents

Contents

Contents

8 Your Legacy

9 Resource Guide

Contents

FOREWORD

The Great Spirit must have loved stories
Because the Great Spirit made many people.

INUIT SAYING

Cross-culturally, storytelling is the oldest teaching and healing art that is used for purposes of transmitting values, history, teachings, and life skills. Every human being is filled with stories. Behind each of the following questions is a story to be told: What is the funniest thing that has ever happened to you? What was the most creative endeavor in which you have been involved? Who are the people who taught you about love? What was the first unforgettable spiritual experience you had? What was the most challenging experience of your life? What was the strangest thing that ever happened to you?

Stories illustrate truths, give us examples to live by, entertain us, teach us the meaning of life, and carry us into the mystery. What do all of the stories we hear have in common? They contain universal truths, aspects of life with which we can all identify. Stories hold meaning for us; they call forth memories and ignite our imaginations. They contain points or lessons that are either drawn from the past or pulled from the future, so that we can continually move forward in the present. Every family and organization has stories. What are yours?

Living Legacies is an invaluable resource for helping us cull stories, events, people, turning points, and unforgettable moments. One of the greatest gifts we can give is to leave a memoir or creative legacy of what inspired, challenged, surprised, and touched us during our lives. Friends, colleagues, and loved ones avidly learn from our triumphs and failures. Duane Elgin and Coleen LeDrew show us a way we can all track the meaningful and heartfelt moments in our lives. From male and female perspectives, they provide a map that shows us how we can track, revisit, and integrate more fully the joys, sorrows, learnings, and blessings that life and relationships continue to offer us.

This exceptional and comprehensive guidebook makes it possible for us to uncover and discover the courageous and compelling stories in our lives and provides a testament and legacy to the majestic challenge and beauty found in each human being's sacred journey through life.

—Angeles Arrien, Ph.D.,
cultural anthropologist and author
of *The Four-Fold Way*, *Signs of Life*,
and *The Nine Muses: A Mythological
Path to Creativity*

1

WHY CREATE STORIES?

Everybody has a story to tell. The trouble is, these days people don't believe their stories are worth much. But we have to tell our stories; otherwise, how are we going to know who we are? We have to listen to the stories of other people: how else are we going to know who they are?

STEVEN KENT

Tucked away in a closet or drawer, you probably have a box of old, yellowed photographs—images of earlier times, faces, and occasions that you now only dimly remember, if you remember them at all. Perhaps there are names and dates on the backs of some of the photos. Who are these people? What were their lives about? What are the stories that go with these pictures?

For millennia, people have been gathering in circles around campfires and at kitchen tables to share stories. It is in our nature to share stories. Yet many of us have all but lost touch with this art. Today we have all sorts of cameras to record the special occasions in our lives, but the photographs and videotapes cannot tell what we felt, how a particular moment changed us, or why it mattered. They do not communicate the way our own stories do.

*E*ach of our lives is an unfolding story, full of characters we feel strongly about and events that alter who we are. Stories are powerful teaching tools because they reflect our lived experience. When people share their experiences in stories, we become active participants in those experiences. Our minds and hearts are engaged as we hear about characters and want to know how it all turns out. Think back to the last lecture you heard. If the lecturer spoke for an hour and in that time included a three-minute story, you most likely remember the story more vividly than anything else. Stories carry important truths that can stay in our memories and impact our lives.

Within each and every person are stories that can teach, inspire, heal, awaken, and reveal universal experiences that connect us with each other. The power of stories is their ability to weave us into relationships with one another by communicating in simple terms the experiences and qualities we share.

Like many people, Elizabeth Share began to wonder about the stories of her ancestors when she was still a teenager. Up to that point, she had enjoyed looking at old family photos but aside from knowing the names of her closest relatives she had little information about life in her family even two generations back. Elizabeth had a copy of the only photograph that existed of her grandmother as a child. Although she had heard snippets of information about the picture, she had never taken the time to ask her grandmother about it. When her grandparents celebrated their fiftieth wedding anniversary, there was a large family reunion, and Elizabeth decided to take the opportunity to learn something about her family's past. She interviewed both her grandparents and tape-recorded the interview. One of the things she asked her grandmother was to describe the day the photo was taken and the memories that it elicited. She was surprised by how much she learned. "I didn't know they had walked so far to have the picture taken. I didn't know how her brother had died. I didn't know very much at all."

Elizabeth made copies of the taped stories for the rest of her family. "My family couldn't believe how fabulous it was that we had gotten these stories. It was incredible how much joy everyone got from hearing them."

At the time, Elizabeth did not fully understand the value of the stories she had collected. "When my grandmother was alive, the impact of her stories did not really hit me. My youth and inexperience got in the way." Years later, Elizabeth found her appreciation deepening for her grandmother's life and the stories she had told. "I started to think about where I came from, who I was, and what I would teach my children. I realized that unless I made a conscious effort to share our family history with the children, much would be forgotten, and so much would be lost." Now Elizabeth considers her grandmother's photograph and the story about it among her most precious possessions. "I want my children to have the photograph and the story. I hope that when they are older, they will write about the photograph and the important place it had in our home."

A single story about the family matriarch became not only a gift to Elizabeth's relatives and later her own children, but also a touchstone that links Elizabeth with her past and reminds her—more and more as she matures—of what is important in her life. Here is Elizabeth's story with the photograph of her grandmother as a girl and a pressed rose that once belonged to Merke. Elizabeth's grandmother, Merke, is second from the right.

Remembering Merke

by Elizabeth Share

I thought I knew her. It wasn't until after her death that I realized how much I had assumed and how little I really understood.

"If only I could tell you what I have seen," she would say. To which I would answer, "Grandma, you've told me a million times."

My grandmother was a devoted woman whose features were plain and whose figure was sturdy. Her eyes lacked sparkle, her ankles were thick, and her teeth were those of a woman who'd been too poor for dental care. Grandma wore musty-smelling flowered housecoats and terry-cloth slippers; she padded unambitiously about her tiny apartment. I remember sneaking in to see her dress one morning when I was about six and laughing with my sister at the way her heavy breasts hung shapelessly to her waist. We watched her trying to cradle them into her bra, and we faulted her for becoming so unappealingly wilted.

My grandfather says she was a beauty when he met her. "A real looker," he said. She had beautiful long blonde hair, and, though I have never seen evidence of this, he says she had a beautiful figure.

What I have seen is a picture of her as a child in Poland. She is posed formally with her mother and siblings. They had walked eight hours through the forest to reach a man who took photographs so they could send one to her father in America. She was an ethereally beautiful child, her face wise and prematurely solemn.

I kept this photo on my dresser, and each time she saw it she pointed out the same two details. The first was that the hem had fallen on her skirt, an embarrassment that had occurred on the long walk from her village to town. The threadbare fabric had caught on a bush, and that unkempt hem screamed poverty to her. She asked me more than once to put the photo away so no one would see it. The second detail she lamented was the image of the smallest child in the photo, little Aaron, who had been kicked in the head by a horse and died before he was four. "We didn't have no doctors then," she cried. "We didn't have so much as a piece of bread to give him."

She tried to tell me of the sorrows that had begun so early to bear down on her heart—the poverty and responsibility and hunger—but all I usually said was, "Grandma, can't you ever say anything nice about your childhood?"

I cringe now to think I understood so little. And I am eternally grateful that she told and retold her story to me even when it seemed to fall on deaf ears. I cry for all the years I managed not to hear the stories she had to tell, and now I cry for the beautiful voice I hear in my head repeating those stories while I listen and listen and listen.

Recording and sharing our stories is one of the most profound gifts we can give. There's the gift we give when we invite others to tell us their stories, and we collect and preserve them. As it was in Elizabeth's case, we honor the storytellers with our interest (this is especially profound when they are elders), the stories we collect are a blessing to others now and in future generations, and we inevitably learn far more from the experience than we expect. Stories also record and preserve special moments in our children's lives and become lasting reminders of their tenderness, curiosity, and innocence. When we record our life experiences, we also give the gift of letting others know who we are. When we share our thoughts and feelings, the important moments in our lives, and how we came to be who we are today, those who read or hear our stories will know not only us better but themselves as well. That's because sharing experiences reflects that which is most human and universal in each of us. Stories also bestow gifts on ourselves: it is a gift to create, to remember, to take time for introspection, to reflect on what matters most, and to bring together the forgotten threads of our personal histories.

Creating Your Life Stories

Although it's meaningful and even profound to collect the stories of friends and relatives, your own stories are particular treasures. Collecting them is not only a gift for others, but also it can be a wonderful process of reflection for you. You can reflect on your life and what matters most to you; share what has touched, changed, or moved you; express something you have never revealed before; and celebrate and remember the miracle of life. Whether the story is about your childhood; a turning point in your life; important people, places, and events; or something funny that happened to you, it can capture the essence of a time in your life and its meaning for you today.

Reflecting on your personal stories can be a transformational experience. In creating your stories, you have an opportunity to explore, discover, and create a record of what you care about, what touches you, and where your passions lie. In doing so, you may discover new insights into what matters most to you. Pat Tyler, whose story begins on page 154, found that writing and sharing her stories about Vietnam helped her come to terms with her experience of the war and realize her deep commitment to peace. By revealing yourself authentically, you will naturally bring to life remarkable stories. You may also discover what you want your legacy to be—what you want to pass on from your life to future generations.

Our Approach to Recording Stories

There are many ways to record stories, including scrapbooking, digital storytelling on a computer, tape recordings, videotaping, journal entries, memoirs, essays, musings, and reminiscences. Each way has value.

The approach we suggest here is distinct from all of these. We call it the *life story*. It is a short, written story, accompanied by visual images, in which you take the reader on a journey into particular events of your own or your subject's life. Together you will feel, discover, and reflect on the meaning of this life story.

We recommend written stories because they involve a greater depth of reflection and have an enduring quality. The written word is powerful. Barbara Easterlin, whose story begins on page 86, describes the experience recording her stories this way: "Writing stories makes me think about my experience more deeply—the essence of it. I reach down and look at what's going on in my heart." Cynthia Schuetz, whose story begins on page 90, explains it like this: "Something happens when I write that doesn't happen when I talk. I can touch places that I think I can touch only when I write. Even when I speak my truth and strive to be honest, when I speak it's different than when I write it."

We also suggest that you use visual elements that will bring your story even more alive. By combining your writing with photographs and other illustrations, your story page can express the richly textured array of thoughts and feelings that your story evokes.

There are advantages to recording your stories in this way. A life story can be short and simple, yet it can recreate an experience in such a way that it takes the reader and you on a journey into the events of your life.

A Life Story Can Be Short and Simple

Simple stories can be unexpectedly powerful. That is why the suggestions in this book are geared toward creating short, one- to two-page, life stories that are combined with photographs and other images. We focus on those vivid experiences that represent important turning points in our lives because of the way they make us see our world and ourselves differently as a result. You can, however, adapt the suggestions in this book to different forms of writing. For example, instead of a short life story, you may want to write a letter to your children, transcribe an interview with your grandfather, or write extended passages about your life.

The stories you create can be simple in content but rich in depth or detail—how you met your beloved partner, the first time you swam in the ocean, your trip overseas. Or they can be more elaborate stories that describe a lifelong recurring fear or longing, a transformational relationship, or even something still unresolved. What you choose to write about is not nearly as important as that you care about your subject and are moved to share the experience.

A Life Story Can Recreate the Experience

In chapter 4, we provide guidance for making your writing as engagingly vivid as possible. Tales told well convey the spirit of the event. With great attention to the details, they transport us to the felt experience of the place and the characters. They recreate the experience for us. We feel like we are there. The exercises in this book will help you write stories that bring the reader into your world to live with and learn from you. In this way, life stories pass on history and meaning. They touch our hearts, help us bond, and make us laugh, cry, and remember that we are not alone.

A Story Is a Journey

Imagine reading a story written by your grandmother about the day she and your grandfather were married. You may enjoy reading about your grandmother's thoughts about marriage, but her reflections would probably have more meaning in the context of a story. For example, a story about how she forgave your grandfather for losing the wedding ring may capture the character of their relationship, or a story about the little touches that turned a camping trip into a romantic honeymoon could show what she loved about him. In writing your life stories, you are not only bringing your reader with you on a journey. You are embarking on your own journey, reflecting on memories of your experiences, and making meaning from your life.

The Purpose of This Book

Whether you already have a folder full of family stories or are mystified about what your stories might be, this book can be your guide to writing, illustrating, collecting, and preserving your life stories. By using this book, you can uncover the seeds of stories in your life, follow a simple process for writing them, and learn techniques for illustrating your stories with photographs and other images. We offer questions for you to consider that will help draw out your stories and those of your family and friends. You'll also find sample stories that present a variety of ideas, styles, and techniques.

Your life is full of experiences that are stories waiting to be told. As you uncover your own treasure chest of stories, you will have an opportunity to explore aspects of your life you may not have thought to consider and to enroll your family and friends in participating with you. Whether you ultimately create a scrapbook of your own stories, a collection of stories with your family, or just one story for a special occasion, you will have created a priceless treasure that will become even more cherished as the years go by.

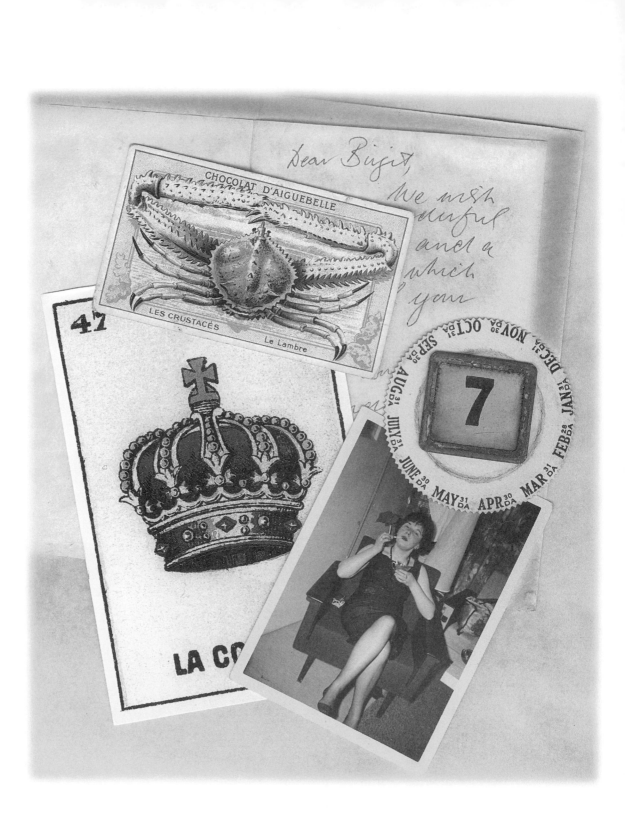

2
HOW TO BEGIN

*When we seek for connection, we restore the world to whole-
ness. Our seemingly separate lives become meaningful as we
discover how truly necessary we are to each other.*

MARGARET WHEATLEY

There are a number of important things to consider before you begin. Although it may seem premature, one of the first things you need to think about is what you intend to do with your stories. That's because your purpose and your intended audience will determine what you choose to write about and the look and feel of the finished story. You also want to think about whether to involve others in the process, how to keep track of your ideas and materials, and the materials and tools you will need. Given the fast pace of today's life with all of its demands, it may be difficult to make time for your creative process. So we begin by considering how creating life stories can become a part of your life.

Making Time for Your Stories

You may be wondering how you can find the time to create and collect stories. We suggest that you set aside a specific time to work on your stories—perhaps once a day, once a week, or whenever works best for you. Pick a time when you can minimize interruptions and focus on what you are creating. By developing your stories over time—doing a little every day, week, month, or even every year—you make the project doable. Another approach is to schedule "story time" during special periods throughout the year, such as the three days after Thanksgiving, the last week of the year, or during a vacation or a family reunion. These would be particularly good times if you would like to include family members or friends in the process. For example, you could invite people to share stories during holiday dinners or other gatherings of family and friends.

That said, the best advice we can give is to start by having your goal be to complete just one story. It is better to complete one than to give up after becoming overwhelmed because you attempted too much. This is one project where quality is far more important than quantity.

Why Create This Story?

To create a life story, the place to begin is with your intention for the finished creation. Knowing why you are creating a story and who it is for will guide you in selecting a topic, what and how you write about it, how you illustrate it, and what you do with your story once it's complete. In short, it will impact every aspect of this process.

Start by asking yourself what you want your finished creation to be and who is it for. One possibility is to create a story album that you can share with friends and family as you would a photo album. Or you could create a story or a collection of stories for a specific purpose, such as to give as a gift for your mother's seventieth birthday, to give to a couple for their wedding or anniversary, or to serve as a memorial to a departed friend. You could also create a story as a keepsake of a special occasion, such as your child's first day of school (this would make a terrific gift for grandparents) or a trip overseas.

Another possibility is to create a collection of stories with a broader range and purpose—perhaps the important experiences in your child's life, the stories of your parents and grandparents to distribute among your family, or your personal stories to pass on to future generations. You might even choose to create life stories for your own exploration and discovery, and wait until a later time to decide if you want to share them.

If you are creating a story about yourself to later share with others, your focus may be on deeply exploring the meaning of your experience, how you changed because of it, or how it pulls together the many threads of your life. If you are creating a story as a way to honor someone, your focus may be on examples that show how the person made a difference in your life or what you appreciate about him or her. If you are recording a story about your children, you may want to focus on the vivid details of their experience growing up—what they said and did, what was happening at the time, and your reflections on them.

Take some time to reflect on what the purpose of your story is and who the audience will be. You may have a different purpose for each story you develop or you may have only one intention. Once you have completed a story or two, your intentions may expand or shift as you discover new purposes for creating and sharing your life stories.

How to Include Family and Friends

Storytelling is a community activity. Much of the enjoyment and meaning of creating stories comes from sharing our experience with others. While your writing will at some point require you to spend time alone, including others in the process is fun and will bring you closer to friends and family. This can be an interesting and rewarding way to spend time with the people you love, while accomplishing something that you care about. You might want to form a group to share story ideas, or partner with one other person with whom you meet on a regular basis to support one another. There are many ways to share the process and the completed stories with others. Here are a few ideas.

JOIN WITH OTHERS WHO ARE CREATING STORIES

Have you ever noticed how a task that seems overwhelming when done alone can become effortless and enjoyable when done in a group? One way to bring the support and energy of a group to the life-story process is to create a story circle. This is a group (it can even be as simple as you and another person) that meets weekly, biweekly, or monthly to exchange ideas and share your creations. Having a set time to share what you're creating with others will help keep you motivated. You can meet to share supplies and techniques, to give each other feedback on editing and content, to help each other create visual layouts, and to figure out what to do next. Story circles work well for those who want to develop their own stories yet share the process of creation with others.

Another idea is to host a potluck dinner to which people bring a story to share as well as something to eat. Swapping stories with another person or a group can be fun and a good way to expand your storytelling ideas and skills. You can tape-record and later transcribe the stories, or take turns taking notes, recording powerful words and phrases that the teller can use afterward. You might tell stories around specific themes, such as the first time you fell in love, a person who's had a big impact on your life, or an experience that shifted your perspective. (For more ideas on themes, see chapter 5, "Discovering Your Life Stories.")

CREATE A BOOK OF STORIES WITH OTHERS

Another way to participate with others is to have a group create a collection of stories. This could be a book created by a family, a couple, or a group of friends— perhaps as a special present for a dear friend's birthday, for a wedding, or for a teenager going off to college. You could create a group book by having the group create stories together or by having each person create a story. If you invite others to contribute a story to a collection, it may be helpful to provide them with some support materials, such as some guidance regarding the writing process, a sample story or two, and a few ideas for topics.

One of the challenges of creating a group book is that there is only one original copy (with original photographs). If you are making a book of stories to share among the group, it is important that the participants agree up front on who will keep the original and how it will be passed on to future generations. Then you can make color copies of the story pages and give a set to each participant. Even though copies will fade faster than a photograph, they can provide a good short-term solution. Perhaps the best way to save and store multiple copies is to digitize the stories by scanning and storing them on a disk. They can then be printed at a later time with a color printer.

INVITE FAMILY AND FRIENDS TO CREATE STORIES FOR YOUR COLLECTION

Whether or not your family and friends create their own stories, you can still invite them to participate in creating yours. For example, you might ask them to contribute something to include in your book, such as a story about an experience they had with you, a quote or poem that describes how they feel about you, or any story about them that they would like to share with you. Give several suggestions and let them decide. You might also interview a member of your family or a friend (see "Interviewing Family and Friends for Great Stories" on page 116). With interesting questions, an interview can lead to juicy insights and unexpected gems that can be turned into a story, or you can include a transcription of the interview in your book.

How to Keep Track of Your Ideas

*A*s you get further into the process of recording stories, you will probably find yourself thinking frequently of ideas for stories, often at odd times and places. It may be helpful to keep a notebook or journal handy so that you can record your ideas and stories all in one place. If you plan to write your stories on a computer, it's a good idea to create a special directory to keep track of your notes and ideas. Another approach is to use 3 x 5 cards. You can write each story idea on a different 3 x 5 card and later sort through the cards to organize your writing. Or you may find it helpful to organize your materials in individual file folders. You can create a file for each story topic. As you collect ideas, photographs, letters, and quotes, you can easily slip them into the appropriate file.

How to Record Your Stories

*A*fter you decide the type of stories you intend to create, who they are for, and whether and how to have other people participate, your next decision will be to select the medium you want to use. In this section, we present some things to be aware of as you make that choice.

SCRAPBOOKS

This book offers instructions for creating life stories that are created and stored scrapbook style—on paper in a book or binder. You can easily adapt most of our suggestions, however, to create and store your stories on a computer hard drive or disk. We have chosen the scrapbook approach because it allows you to create a book of any length, is easiest to use, requires no special technical know-how, and supplies are easy to obtain. If you use a scrapbook, you can later store your photographs or even all your pages on a computer disk simply by scanning them in. More information about scrapbooks can be found in chapter 9.

ACID-FREE MATERIALS

Whether you use a scrapbook or not, we assume that you will want to include photographs and other visuals in your stories. If you create only written stories, the supplies you will need will be very simple—paper, pen, and a typewriter or computer. If you create illustrated stories, we recommend that you use only acid-free materials, including paper, pens, and paste to help preserve your photographs and story pages. Further information about protecting your photographs and using acid-free materials can be found in chapter 7.

AUDIO AND VIDEOTAPES

You also might want to consider using an audiotape or videotape to accompany your stories. Narrating one or more of your stories on tape adds to their intimacy, and allows those who listen to it to have much more of a sense of you. We recommend that you include a paper copy of anything that is on a cassette or a disk in case there is a technical problem or the technology becomes outdated.

Supplies for the Scrapbook Approach

Here are the basic supplies that you will need to create stories that will be stored scrapbook style:

- A binder, scrapbook, or journal with acid-free pages
- Acid-free paper in a variety of colors, textures, and weights
- Acid-free glue or tape
- Acid-free pens (available in a variety of colors and point sizes)
- Photographs, keepsakes, and other visual props
- Scissors and ruler

In addition to these basic supplies, you may also need or want to have these materials and tools on hand:

- Acid-free plastic sheet covers or Mylar covers
- Precision knife, personal trimmer, or other fine paper-cutting tool
- Double-sided acid-free tape
- A camera and film
- A tape recorder with a microphone and blank audiocassette tapes
- A video camera and videocassettes
- A computer and printer, or a typewriter
- Access to a photocopy machine

Storing all your acid-free paper, pens, glue, and cutting tools in a box will make it easy to access what you need when you are ready to create.

Using a Computer

There are many advantages to using a computer to write your stories: the text is easy to read and you can fit more text on a page, format the text in different ways, make changes easily, and store what you create on a disk.

If you have a computer, access to a scanner, and a software program with graphics capabilities, you can create stories, complete with photographs and other images, on-line. They can then be displayed on a Web page and transmitted over the Internet to friends and family using e-mail. Importantly, digital images will not degrade over time as long as the storage device is sound. Chapter 7, which focuses on using visual images, provides additional information about and examples of using computers to create stories.

Using a computer to work with text and graphics also enables you to do "digital storytelling." This approach combines digital images, text, video footage, and voice to create digital stories that are displayed on a computer screen and are viewable on Web pages. As computer technology advances, and the cost of computer equipment and software decreases, the tools for digital storytelling will become increasingly widely available. Chapter 9 lists some Web sites that provide information on digital story-telling.

Despite all these advantages, you may not want to use a computer to write your stories. With pen and paper you provide a personal touch. Like everything else having to do with creating your life stories, your choice of format will make your finished product uniquely yours.

3

CREATING YOUR TIME LINE

Stories knit together the realities of past and future,
of dreamed and intended moments. They teach us
how we perceive and why we wonder.

JOAN HALIFAX

If you are bursting with ideas for stories and ready to begin writing, you may want to jump right to the next chapter. But if you do not have specific stories in mind or would like to uncover more, then you will probably find this chapter useful. It explains how to create a time line of significant events or experiences in your life that can help you discover valuable seeds of stories, which you can then nurture and grow.

Your time line will allow you to review the many potential stories from your life. It can serve as a tool for inspiring story ideas, and you can refer back to it later as you explore and develop ideas. You can even include your time line in your collection of stories. You can make it simple or complex. The choice is yours.

To make your time line, you'll need a large piece of paper. We suggest that you tape together two or three 8.5 x 11-inch sheets so that you have enough area to work. Before doing anything else, take a look at the sample time line on pages 46. It was created by a friend of ours, Genevieve "Gen" Tyler, with the help of her daughter Pat Tyler.

As Gen did on hers, draw a line across the length of your paper. Leave some room at the top and bottom to fill in information. At the left end of the line, mark your birth with the date and a symbol that indicates the beginning. Write the names of people who were in your life at birth (such as parents and siblings) and where you lived. Then indicate ten-year periods across the time line and have it end with your age today. Then write in significant events and experiences. The lists below will give you some ideas about which events and experiences from your life you might want to include.

Consider including in your time line important events from your life such as these:

- Births and deaths
- Moves to new homes
- Marriage and divorce
- Beginnings of important relationships—friends, lovers, mentors, animals
- Starting and graduating from school
- Job changes

- Accidents and injuries
- Special trips, visits, vacations
- Turning points such as discovering your independence, leaving home, joining an important organization

Also consider for your time line what significant experiences you have had, such as the following:

- First times that were important to you, such as when you first went to school, learned to play an instrument, lived on your own, traveled to another country, fell in love, got a job
- Memories of the most painful, joyful, funny, stressful, triumphant, or powerful times of your life
- Heart openings, such as unexpected acts of compassion or kindness, or your awareness of the suffering of others
- Small and not-so-small miracles, such as an unexplainable healing, unusual synchronicities, intuitions, or a dream that foretold the future
- Life-changing experiences, such as a major shift in your spiritual beliefs, a profound moment of awakening, mystical experiences
- World events that impacted your life, such as the Vietnam War, the assassination of John F. Kennedy or of Martin Luther King, Jr., the landing of the first man on the moon, the AIDS epidemic, the Challenger explosion, the fall of the Berlin Wall

After you've looked over these lists, create your list of important events and significant experiences in your life. Then place on your time line key words, symbols, or illustrations to signify each. For example, you might draw a heart and inside it write the name of a romantic partner to indicate each significant love in your life. For both events and experiences, include the names of people who were a significant part of what happened. These may include family, friends, important teachers or mentors, spouses, and colleagues.

To help you recall events, you might ask people who know you well if they remember important events, achievements, and changes in your life. To find out their perspective on your past, ask what they remember about you and your family.

After you have filled in your time line, go back and review it. Which items bring up the most vivid memories, images, or feelings? Which have a story just waiting to be told? Which contain the seeds for stories that you will need to reflect on to enable them to grow? You may want to color code your time line by circling items that bring up vivid memories in red, those that have stories that you can easily write in blue, and those containing the seeds of stories that will take nurturing to develop in green. After you have finished your time line, keep it handy so you can refer back to it as you work on your stories.

If you plan to save your time line as part of your collection of stories, consider adding to it photographs, images, letters, keepsakes, and newspaper clippings that portray or expand on the information you recorded.

If you want to record the stories of others, you may want to help them create time lines. The longer people have lived, the more daunting the task can seem. Keep it simple by drawing out the topics and turning points that people are most interested in or most want to share. Ask them to show you photographs and keepsakes that may help them recall events and places that were significant in their lives.

Barbara Easterlin, the author of "Letter to Emma and Ryder" on page 86, suggested that parents of small children might want to construct a time line of developmental firsts, such as the first time the child sat up, first steps, first words, and the first day of school. A developmental time line can help you recall some of the precious moments in your children's lives and can serve as a visual story of their early years. You can add photographs and other items and use colorful markers to make it playful.

On the following page is Genevieve Tyler's time line. Gen sprinkled the pages with photographs and included a phrase under each event that would help her recall a story about her experience.

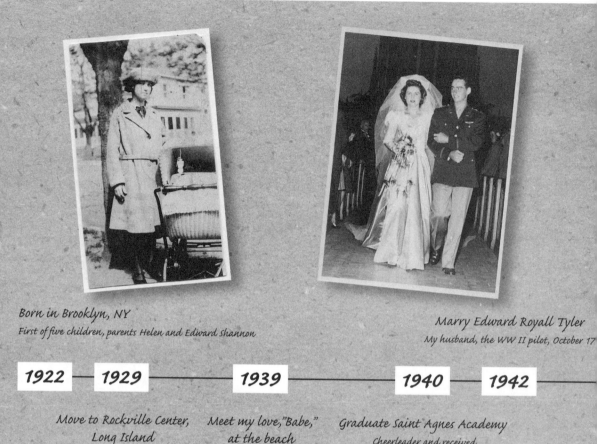

Born in Brooklyn, NY
First of five children, parents Helen and Edward Shannon

Marry Edward Royall Tyler
My husband, the WW II pilot, October 17

1922 — **1929** ——————— **1939** ——————————————— **1940** — **1942** ———

Move to Rockville Center,
Long Island

Meet my love, "Babe,"
at the beach
I was 16, he was 19

Graduate Saint Agnes Academy
*Cheerleader and received
history & English medals*

Work at World's Fair

*Genevieve Shannon Tyler
My Life's Time Line*

GEN - WORLDS FAIR

End of WW II
Pat's words, "The war is over, my
daddy is coming home."

Lots of parties 1950s
Christmas house with Santa
Growing a family

First grandchild,
Melissa, is born
I'm a grandmother, what a thrill!

1945 ——————— **1950s** ——— **1968** —— **1976** ———

1943, Birth of daughter Pat

1947, Birth of son Edward

1950, Birth of daughter Diane

1951, Birth of daughter Kathleen

1956, Birth of son Jeffrey

1963, Birth of daughter Lisa
A surprise and what a joy!

Pat serves in Vietnam
One-star flag in the window

Mom dies
Lost a dear friend,
a little birdy told me

Dog and cat die

Pilgrimage to
Medjugorje, Yugoslavia
Spiritual journey to peace

Move to California,
living alone for first time
I am stronger than I had thought

| 1984 | 1985 | 1987 | 1988 | 1989 |

Dad dies

Lisa and Mark marry
Unity of family –
East and West Coast

My "Babe,"
Edward, dies
suddenly

Run first race – 10K
I did it!

Become an
Eucharistic minister
Does your church
buy your clothes?

My life -
what a blessing!

The ambulance ride to the hospital
Beet-juice incident, survived nicely!

Eric Royall is graduating from college
First grandchild to graduate, my grandson the dentist

1990s   **1999**   **2000**

Family Sundays at the beach
What would I do without you all?

Arrival twelfth grandchild
She came from China

4

WRITING YOUR LIFE STORIES

We write to taste life twice, in the moment, and in retrospection. . . .
We write to be able to transcend our life, to reach beyond it.
We write to teach ourselves to speak with others,
to record the journey into the labyrinth.

ANAÏS NIN

As you approach the task of creating a story, you may be feeling many things— excitement, anxiety, bewilderment, inspiration. It's natural. Our lives are complex and have rich layers of experience that are sometimes difficult to convey. We are on a journey of continual transformation. On this journey, we let go, open up, close down, forgive, forget, embrace, get caught, contract, expand, regret, and celebrate ourselves and our lives. It can be a challenge even to think of capturing this richness on paper. When we try, the results may sometimes be skillful and at other times awkward. Anytime we try to express ourselves, we face the challenge of giving form to something that exists only in our hearts and minds.

Don't worry about doing it right. Your stories are for you first of all. So have fun. You can't do it wrong. Your friends and relatives who may eventually read your stories would probably tell you the same. If you receive a letter from a friend or family member, does it matter if it's not perfectly written? What matters is the generosity of spirit and love that motivated the person to reach out and share with you. That is what you will be giving your readers. They care about you sharing your experiences, not whether your writing is perfect.

You can tell a story in many different ways, all interesting and meaningful, so allow yourself to feel the freedom and opportunity that comes with creating. Explore with curiosity the stories that you know about and the ones that you discover. Let this process of reflecting on your life experience deepen your inner wisdom and rejuvenate your creativity and aliveness. Celebrate your stories and the process of telling them.

Finding Your Voice and Style

It is important to anchor your writing in your own voice and style. Most experiences that we want to share are very telling in and of themselves. Although you may need to reflect on your story to undercover its meaning, you don't have to write in any particular style to make it significant. Keep it simple and trust that your experience is enough to hold a reader's interest. Simplicity will allow substance to show through.

When you begin to write, imagine that you are speaking with a dear friend or relative, either now or in the future. When you bring that sort of intimacy to your writing, your readers will feel it. If it's helpful, visualize yourself speaking to your imagined listener and notice how you want to tell your story. Pay attention to details—feelings, tone or mood, setting, and reflections that convey your experience.

Making It Personal

*I*n your stories, you are often the central character as well as the creator. To express your experience, it helps to be open about yourself. As you look at which experiences you could write about, consider the joy and the grief; times when you were strong and others when you were vulnerable; the moments you are proud of and those that were difficult. Overcoming challenges or living with adversity is often what shapes our identity and helps us ultimately find enjoyment in life. Moreover, everybody makes mistakes. Our willingness to show our imperfections and share embarrassing or painful moments enables others to connect with us. Your readers will feel closer to you and enjoy reading your stories if you reveal the full spectrum of your humanity.

In creating your stories, you have an opportunity to explore parts of yourself that you may not have expressed before. In the process, you may discover your edges—the places where you find it uncomfortable to share. Most of us have experiences, feelings, and parts of ourselves that we keep hidden from others. In certain situations, it can be appropriate and even wise to choose not to share something. Other times, it can be healing to tell the truth without shame or blame. If you are not sure whether or not to share something, ask yourself whether revealing it would be hurtful to yourself or another. If so, do not share it. If it would bring healing, consider including it.

Choosing a Topic

*B*y now you probably have one or more story ideas in mind. Which one are you most drawn to? That's the one to write about. Your story will be most effective and you will have the most fun writing it if you pick the topic that you care most about. Record the story that you find exciting, that captivates your interest, and with which you have the most direct experience.

If you can't think of a story idea, see "There's a First Time for Everything" on the next page or explore some of the topics in chapter 5 for ideas.

Allow Your Story to Blossom

*O*nce you have selected a topic, find some quiet space where you can concentrate and create. It helps to bring your full attention to the writing process. Take a moment to relax and center yourself before you begin. Breathe. Give yourself some quiet time to reflect. Let go of thoughts about your day and other distractions. Let go of your inner critic.

You may find that much of your story comes to you when you're not trying to write it. It may come while you are walking, commuting to work, showering, dreaming, or daydreaming. Nurture your stories by giving them the time they need to unfold.

There's a First Time for Everything

First-time experiences often stand out in our memories because of our excitement and curiosity when we do something new and because we are no longer the same person after the experience. As a result, they are potent seeds for stories.

Write a list of some of the significant "first times" in your life. When was the first time you fell in love? Spoke in front of an audience? Traveled to another country? To help jog your memory, we have listed below a few examples of firsts that include both the event and a possible story theme or outcome. You could write about the first time you:

- Visited your family's homeland and learned something about a grandparent.
- Met someone special and felt that your life was about to change forever.
- Camped in the wilderness and were in awe of the night sky.
- Accepted a challenging job and surprised yourself with how well you did.
- Swam in a lake and overcame your fear of deep water.

What other first times come to mind? For each idea, jot down the key words that trigger the memory of the experience. Once you have listed a few possibilities, review your list and see if one stands out as particularly funny, significant, or memorable. If there is more than one, pick the one you think would be the most fun to write about.

Putting Pen to Paper

*E*ach story you write will go through a process of development and refinement. Most people rewrite their stories a number of times. You may develop a draft, set it aside, ask others for feedback, and then revise your story. The process we suggest has seven basic steps. The steps you go through in developing your story will vary depending on your unique approach, your writing style, the story content, and how you involve others.

STEP ONE: VISUALIZE THE STORY

When you are ready to write, a good way to begin is to sit quietly and play the story in your mind like a film. Review as much of the episode as you can, noticing the details. What images do you see? What smells, sounds, tastes, and textures do you experience? What emotions do you feel? Go over the story a few times so that you can recall it fully.

STEP TWO: CREATE A FIRST DRAFT

Describe your experience in writing from beginning to end as if telling the story to a friend. Just let it flow spontaneously, without attempting to edit yourself. If you prefer, you can tape-record yourself and then transcribe it. If you're not sure where the story begins, start with the first thing you can think of that led to the experience or start in the middle, then write everything you can remember. If you're stuck and can't even begin to write, try one or more of the suggestions in the box on the next page, "What to Do if You're Stuck."

What to Do if You're Stuck

If you're having trouble with the initial development of your story, you may want to try one or more of these approaches:

- To activate your creativity, write a list of all the words, phrases, quotes, and descriptions related to the experience that you can think of.
- Spend five to ten minutes writing whatever comes to mind about the experience in a continuous, uncensored flow. Then read what you wrote and underline the parts that stand out.
- Record yourself telling the story. It may be helpful to have a friend present to whom you can tell it. Then write out a transcription of the tape. This will be the first draft of your story.
- Tell the story to a friend. Ask your friend to take notes as you speak or to interview you to help uncover the details and meaning of your story.
- Try to develop your opening line first and then fill in the rest of the story. Or develop your concluding sentence first and see how the rest of the story can support that conclusion.
- Set your story aside for a few days and then take a fresh look at it. Taking a break can give you a new perspective.
- Spend twenty to thirty minutes a day developing your story until it flows.
- If you still feel stuck, you may want to choose another story to record. You can come back to your original selection later.

Any story we care about is certain to have layers of meaning and cross-woven themes. This step in the writing process is designed to help you mine through these layers to reveal the most potent nuggets of meaning, what we call the story's gem. If you feel strongly about sharing a story, there is certain to be a gem in it. We call this the "gem" because, as you begin to discover this essence of the story, there's a sense of something shining through. That does not mean that every story has to have an earth-shattering punch line. A gem can be found in lighthearted discoveries as much as poignant moments. As you develop your story, keep an eye out for the glint of this gem. It will help guide you in determining which details to add, what to emphasize, and what to remove. It is not always clear, however, what the main theme is when you start recording your story. The following process will help you discover it.

Once you've written the first draft, underline key words or phrases that are powerful and seem to reveal the heart of the story. Read it through and ask yourself: What is this story about? How am I different now because of the experience? How has my view of the world, another person, or myself changed because of this experience? Write down some possible answers to each question. There are almost always many levels to a story and various meanings for each level. List as many as you'd like. For example, the same story could be about discovering your ability to trust someone, learning an ethical lesson, and uncovering the power of your heart to forgive.

Read through your list of answers. To which one are you drawn the most? In which are you most interested? At this point, consider the answer you pick to be your gem, regardless of whether it is jumping out of the story or you have only a vague feeling about it right now.

Your own interest is the best compass for determining the meaning of your story. If you are still unsure of the main theme, however, this is a great time to ask a friend to read the story aloud to you. Other people can bring an objectivity we lack when we are too close to the material. As you listen to the story being read to you, consider its meaning to you. Then ask what your friend thinks the story is about and what would help bring out the meaning. Be aware that feedback can sometimes feel like criticism, even when it's given gently. Our stories are part of us, and we can feel vulnerable when people express their opinions about them. If you do feel vulnerable, ask for feedback only from people who know how to give their comments constructively, or ask the person to give you no feedback but simply ask you questions like "Why is this important to you?" or "What stands out for you as you listen to it?"

If you are still not sure what the heart of your story is, take a break and come back to it. When you have uncovered the gem of your story, you can go to the next step.

Let's take a look at a story and how it was enhanced by finding the gem and making it shine. On the following page is an early draft of a story by Coleen's mom, Elaine.

An Early Draft of Elaine's Story

It was the summer of my thirteenth birthday and I was visiting my aunt and uncle at the seashore. Their cottage was a few blocks from a bay on the Atlantic Ocean. It was early summer and not yet warm enough to go swimming, so I went down to the beach, took my shoes off, and walked, letting the cold water rush over my feet. I loved the feel of the sand. I walked along collecting shiny pebbles and seashells that I would bring back home with me. At the end of the beach was a pier of rocks where I sat soaking up the sun as I watched the waves crash upon the rocks.

The beach had been deserted that day, so I was startled when a voice asked, "I don't suppose this belongs to you?" I looked up to see a young man of eighteen or nineteen holding an old fishing lure. I am sure I blushed when I said, "No." He said he didn't think so, but he wanted to be sure. He then went on to tell me he belonged to the coast guard and that his station was just beyond the rock pier and sand dunes. I had remembered seeing the coast guard station on a walk once before. It had one of those towers with a light signal.

He asked if I came to the beach often and was I here for the summer. I was a bit tongue-tied and felt giddy and awkward at the same time. Realizing I was flustered, I said I'd better get home. I left in a hurry as the man said he hoped to see me here again. As I walked the long stretch of beach back home, my heart slowed down. I laughed at myself, realizing an "older man" was interested in my company. He was trying to engage me, little me, into conversation.

Walking toward my aunt's cottage, I wondered what the rest of the week would bring.

As you can tell from the story, Elaine knows that meeting the young man on the beach was a significant event in her life. She tells the story simply, the way she might say it to a friend, and it works. But it was obvious that something was missing. The main theme was not clear. To uncover the gem in this story, Elaine asked herself, What am I trying to communicate? What is the story about? She then listed some of the possibilities:

- The summer of my thirteenth birthday
- How I love the beach
- Flirting with an older man
- Seeing myself as a woman for the first time

After making this list, Elaine realized that this experience was significant because it was the first time she saw herself as a woman. That is the gem in her story.

STEP FOUR: ADD DETAILS THAT GIVE LIFE TO YOUR STORY

Once you have determined the central meaning of the piece, add details that bring your story to life and give it depth and dimension. What are the details that convey the spirit of the story—a quirky gesture or mannerism, the soft feel and color of grass, the smell of hyacinths coming though the window? Take time to elaborate the details, drawing them out with as much precision as you can muster.

To recreate the experience, place yourself inside it and describe what is happening. For example, instead of saying, "his recovery was miraculous," you might say something like this: I started praying when I saw the doctor walking toward me down the long hall. My heart began to beat faster and everything seemed to be still. When she said, "The cancer is gone," I burst into tears of amazement, and relief filled my heart.

Check to see if details about any of the following will enhance and help develop your story:

- The time and place where the experience occurred
- The colors, sounds, smells, textures, or tastes that were present
- The general atmosphere or mood
- How you felt or what you were thinking
- Descriptions of behaviors, facial expressions, or gestures
- The names of people and places
- Your reflections on the story today
- How the experience has shaped who you are today

One particularly effective way to add details that recreate an experience is to use quoted dialogue from an interview or from your memory of the event. Even a few lines of discourse can enliven a story and capture the essence of an experience. Years later, being able to read the actual words of beloved family members or friends can prove even more precious.

Elaine's draft that appears on page 60 includes a number of details that enhance the story and its central theme. The first paragraph alone is filled with detail. We are told that the story is set during the summer of her thirteenth birthday, in early summer when it was not yet warm enough to go swimming. She was at the seashore, visiting her relatives whose cottage was a few blocks from a bay on the Atlantic. She mentions the cold water and sand under her bare feet, collecting shiny pebbles and seashells, and sitting on the pier in the sun watching the waves crash on the rocks. You can almost smell the ocean because of the details she includes. Later in the story, we meet the young man through the first words he said to her: "I don't suppose this belongs to you." This quote gives us the feeling of being there. Elaine also gives details about how she was feeling, such as that she blushed, her heart slowed down, and she laughed.

One of the most important details to add to your story is a good title. Choose a title that arouses curiosity, sets a mood or tone, or expresses something about the gem of your story without giving it away.

STEP FIVE: TRIM YOUR STORY

We often write far more than is needed to tell a story well. Now that you have added details, this is the time to look through your story for what is redundant, too abstract, or simply irrelevant. As you do this, keep the meaning of your story in mind. Cross out anything that is not relevant to the story's main theme. Doing that is like peeling away layers of distraction so as to reveal the essence. By trimming your story, you can bring into focus the gem that is at the heart of your experience and clear away that which distracts from it. In the process, you may see other details that you want to add to further clarify the point of your story. See the following page for the revisions that Elaine made to her story about seeing herself as a woman for the first time.

Sometimes it is best to wait a day or two after you complete a draft to trim it so that you can look at it freshly. When we are too close to a story, everything in it seems essential.

One technique that may help you find what is not needed is to cut your story by at least half. It's an excellent way to find what your story could live without, even if you end up putting back much of what you cut. Go through the story and cut anything that is not essential. Go ahead, it's only an exercise. Imagine you are an editor who has to shorten the story by half. Put a line through everything you cut. Then read the story in the short-ened version. Are there some sections that now read better? See if you want to keep some of your edits.

End on a note that reinforces the meaning of your story as a whole. Find a point at the end that gives you a feeling of joy, surprise, or completion; that summarizes the gift of the experience; or that captures the spirit of your story. Stop there.

Elaine's Revisions of Her Story

*H*ere are the changes Elaine made to communicate the essence of her story. Words that are underlined are those she added to further develop the story, and those crossed out are what she trimmed.

Beach Blush

It was the summer of my thirteenth birthday and I was visiting my aunt and uncle at the seashore. ~~Their cottage was a few blocks from a bay on the Atlantic ocean. It was early~~

~~summer and~~ <u>Normally, I would have spent the afternoon playing in the water, but this day it was</u> not yet warm enough to go swimming. <u>So I put on my favorite flowered skirt,</u> went down to the beach, took my shoes off, and walked, letting the cold water rush over my feet. I loved the feel of the sand. ~~I walked along collecting shiny pebbles and sea shells that I would bring back home with me.~~ At the end of the beach was a pier of rocks where I sat soaking up the sun as I watched the waves crash upon the rocks.

The beach had been deserted that day, so I was startled when a voice asked, "I don't suppose this belongs to you?" I looked up to see a young man of eighteen or nineteen holding an old fishing lure. <u>At the time, he seemed like an older man to me.</u> I am sure I blushed when I said, "No." He said he didn't think so, but he wanted to be sure. He then went on to tell me he belonged to the coast guard and that his station was just beyond the rock pier and sand dunes. <u>I was taken in by his good looks and sweet smile.</u> ~~I had remembered seeing the coast guard station on a walk once before. It had one of those towers with a light signal.~~

He asked if I came to the beach often and was I here for the summer. I was a bit tongue-tied and felt giddy and awkward at the same time. Realizing I was flustered, I said I'd better get home. I left in a hurry as the man said he hoped to see me here again. As I walked the long stretch of beach back home, my heart slowed down. I laughed at myself, realizing an "older man" was interested in my company. <u>What a surprise!</u> He was trying to engage me, little me, into a conversation. <u>Maybe I wasn't such a little me anymore. Could it be I was becoming a woman?</u>

~~Walking toward my aunt's cottage, I wondered what the rest of the week would bring.~~

STEP SIX: ASK A FRIEND FOR FEEDBACK

After you have completed your story, share it with someone close to you. If you feel comfortable, read it aloud to them. Sharing will give you insights into your story and will entice others to create their own stories along with you.

To give you an opportunity to see your story as others see it, you might want to ask a few questions of anyone who reads it. To get different perspectives, ask more than one person for feedback. Here are several questions that might elicit useful information:

- Where did the story start for you?
- What part of the story interested or captivated you most?
- Was any part confusing? Was anything not clear?
- What could be cut?
- What do you wish was in the story that isn't?
- Was there a point when you became distracted or tuned out?
- What do you want to know more about?
- If the story is about one thing, what would that be?

As others give you their observations on your story, write notes directly on your draft. Be as open to people's comments as possible, but don't feel that you have to make every change that others suggest. It is your story. What's most important is that the story feels authentic to you.

STEP SEVEN: COMPLETING YOUR STORY

After you have integrated others' comments, check grammar, spelling, and punctuation. Look for words or sentences that are awkward or repetitive. Then set your story aside for a day or more. When you are ready, come back to it for one final review.

Remember that your goal is not to write perfectly but to bring your story to life and share your experience with others. What matters most is your unique expression of the experience and its meaning.

Congratulations! You have completed a life story. As you now know, writing one takes time and commitment. Completing just one story is a worthy accomplishment. We hope that the process we describe here has helped make writing your story a little easier and more fun and that you will continue to write stories and share them with your family and friends. The next chapter provides ideas and activities for finding the seeds for stories. Before moving on to that, we suggest that you read the final version of Elaine's story, "Beach Blush," on the next page. Elaine illustrated her story with an old photograph taken of her at the beach the same year as the incident in the story. She also added some of her own drawings of shells to give it a personal touch.

Beach Blush

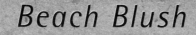

It was the summer of my thirteenth birthday and I was visiting my aunt and uncle at the seashore. Normally, I would have spent the afternoon playing in the water, but this day it was not warm enough to go swimming. So I put on my favorite flowered skirt, went down to the beach, took my shoes off, and walked, letting the cold water rush over my feet. I loved the feel of the sand. At the end of the beach was a pier of rocks where I sat soaking up the sun as I watched the waves crash upon the rocks.

The beach had been deserted that day so I was startled when a voice asked, "I don't suppose this belongs to you?" I looked up to see a young man of eighteen or nineteen holding an old fishing lure. At the time, he seemed like an older man to me. I am sure I blushed when I said, "No." He said he didn't think so, but he wanted to be sure. He then went on to tell me he belonged to the coast guard and that his station was just beyond the rock pier and sand dunes. I was taken in by his good looks and sweet smile.

He asked if I came to the beach often and was I here for the summer. I was a bit tongue-tied and felt giddy and awkward at the same time. Realizing I was flustered, I said I'd better get home. I left in a hurry as the man said he hoped to see me here again. As I walked the long stretch of beach back home, my heart slowed down. I laughed at myself, realizing an "older man" was interested in my company. What a surprise! He was trying to engage me, little me, into a conversation. Maybe I wasn't such a "little me" anymore. Could it be I was becoming a woman?

Elaine le Drew

5

DISCOVERING YOUR LIFE STORIES

*The moment one gives close attention to anything, even
a blade of grass, it becomes a mysterious, awesome,
indescribably magnificent world in itself.*

HENRY MILLER

Life stories begin in our own experience—in those moments when we've been present to life, when we've been inspired, saddened, joyful, contributed to, and mystified. This chapter presents a wide range of topics to inspire you to find your own personal stories. The next chapter presents ideas for developing stories about others and for specific purposes, such as a family history. If you already know the story topic you want to develop, by all means skip over these chapters and get started on your story. But if you don't yet have the story that you want to tell, these chapters are designed to help you recall experiences and give you ideas.

The topics suggested here are only a place to start. Use them as a springboard from which to jump into your own stories. Once you begin to reflect on your life, you may be surprised by how many ideas for stories come to mind.

"The charm, one might say the genius of memory, is that it is choosy,
chancy, and temperamental: it rejects the edifying cathedral and indelibly
photographs the small boy outside, chewing a hunk of melon in the dust."
—Elizabeth Bowen

My Childhood

Childhood memories reveal seeds of our future selves and the conditions that helped make us who we are today. It was as children that we first felt fear and joy, loneliness and belonging. Although for many of us childhood might seem many lifetimes ago, most of us still have vivid memories of particular events and people that shaped our early years. We may remember powerful experiences, such as an illness or accident, as well as such ordinary moments as looking closely at a bug in the garden or smelling soup cooking as we walked into the house. What memories do you recall?

Thinking about familiar places from your childhood can trigger a flood of memories. To recollect childhood experiences, try visualizing your childhood home. Think about the places that you lived from birth until you were an adult. Choose one. Now close your eyes and visualize it. See the front of the house. Notice what you see. What do you hear? Slowly walk up to the front door and go inside. Who is there? What do you smell? Roam around the house and be aware of what you see and feel as you walk from room to room. Go inside your bedroom and look around. What toys and belongings are there? Look out your window. What do you see? What adventures do you remember about your childhood? What important things happened in this home? Return to the front of your home. Take one last look, and open your eyes. Take notes about anything you remembered that contains seeds for future stories.

Often memories are stored in our senses. The smell of certain foods can take us back to our mother's cooking. A song on the radio can remind us of our first love. Explore the sensory details that take you into the experience of your childhood.

The questions below can help further stimulate your memory of your childhood and help garner additional seeds for possible stories:

- Was there a pivotal time in your childhood when everything seemed to change, such as when you moved to another home, got a pet, or started a new school?
- Do you have memories of an important game, music recital, or art project?
- What experiences did you have in nature—trips to a lake or the ocean, camping out under the stars, picnicking in your own backyard?
- Who were the most influential people in your life? What did they teach you?
- Did members of your family face any major challenges, such as loss of a job, a painful divorce, a serious accident, or prolonged illness?
- What rituals were important to your family—special dinners, prayers, or playtimes?
- What was one of the biggest lessons that you learned growing up?
- Do you recall a time when you gained new confidence in yourself?
- Do you remember a time you got into trouble or were scared?

Once you find a topic that engages you, replay the scene in your mind. As you reflect on it, you are likely to remember new levels of memories. You may want to look at the experience from different perspectives—as a lesson, a funny and revealing incident, an existential crisis—and reflect on what impact, if any, it had on your life.

On the next page is the story, "Saving Jenny," by Gwen Gordon in which she describes in detail an experience from her childhood and its impact on her life today.

Saving Jenny

by Gwen Gordon

The summer I turned twelve, I played mother to two orphaned baby squirrels. I named these wiggly pink infants Jimmy and Jenny, and every half-hour I fed them warm formula from a bottle and rubbed their tummies until they pooped. Watching them grow into squirrels through my care was one of the most satisfying experiences I'd had.

As soon as Jimmy and Jenny were old enough to make mischief, I kept them in a big cage, letting them out twice a day to play freely in the house. During playtime, their favorite sports included daredevil leaps onto curtain rods, tap dances on the piano, and mad scampers across high beams. When the squirrels were loose, the rule was all doors and windows had to be closed and the toilet lid shut. One day, at the end of playtime, as usual I called Jimmy and Jenny for their feeding. Normally, both squirrels were easy to coax back for lunch. This time, Jimmy was the only one who came running to perch on top of my head and wait for a walnut. I gave him a few sunflower seed appetizers and called again for Jenny. She was nowhere in sight. I called again, and again, and again. Still no Jenny. I checked under beds, inside closets, laundry baskets, then cabinets, dressers, and curtains. I desperately emptied drawers of clothing and turned over furniture. The heat of motherhood rose in my blood.

Finally, having exhausted every other possibility, I tentatively opened the door to the bathroom. "Oh, no!" It was my worst fear! Bobbing in the unflushed toilet bowl was a gasping, soaking Jenny. I held my breath and pulled her out with my bare hands, wiped her off, and wrapped her in a towel, then ran upstairs yelling for help, "Mom, Dad, Dale, Lynn! HELP!" Dale, my oldest sister, was the only one home. I couldn't remember if we were in the middle of a fight or not. I just blurted out how Jenny had fallen into a bucket of soaking clothes and was drowning when I found her, and couldn't she, Dale, please save her, PLEASE.

Dale had recently been trained as a lifeguard and knew all about first aid for humans. She opened the towel with Jenny's soggy, limp body in it and, without hesitation, covered Jenny's mouth and nose with her mouth and applied mouth-to-squirrel resuscitation. For a few minutes, she tried gently pressing Jenny's belly, then breathing into her, pressing, breathing, pressing, breathing. Gradually the water emptied from Jenny's lungs as Dale's breath filled them. Dale kept breathing and breathing. But after many more rounds, Jenny just lay there, still and breathless. We stared helplessly at her tiny body for what seemed like an eternity. Then Dale and I gravely wrapped her back up in the towel and gave each other a long teary hug.

I don't know if Dale ever suspected that she had applied mouth-to-mouth resuscitation to a squirrel who had been soaking in toilet water. I watched her carefully for the next few days to make sure she didn't get sick. She didn't. In fact, we were both a little better tempered after Jenny's death. We didn't fight nearly as much over who got the bigger serving of dessert or which TV show we were going to watch, and occasionally we even went out of our ways to offer each other a kind word or help with chores. Years later, when I told Dale the truth about the toilet water, she just laughed. It made absolutely no difference to her, she says. She would do it again in a second, maybe after drying Jenny off a little more.

Even though we didn't have the words for it at the time, I think we both felt the supreme honor it was to serve another life so intimately. And, at twelve and sixteen years old, we welcomed the ripening of compassion that was stirred by a helpless squirrel but flowed easily toward each other and eventually, with every year's ripening, a little more toward the rest of the world.

"There are two ways of spreading light:

to be the candle or the mirror that reflects it."

—Edith Wharton

People Who Have Inspired Me

We each have known people who have touched our lives in a way that can only be called a blessing or a gift. Often, their gifts are intangible. They may have given us their wisdom, their love and caring, or their trust. Perhaps they demonstrated a particular quality by their way of being. Duane's father, for example, taught him patience simply by how he did his woodworking. Coleen learned about the value of silence by seeing how her grandmother made time for solitude every morning. These special souls may have passed on to us rituals or traditions, or they may have made us aware that we have a talent that we weren't aware of. Their gifts have become part of us.

You may already have someone in mind that you might like to write about. If you don't, the following suggestions may help you recall people who have inspired you.

- Look through old photographs and keepsakes for the influential people in your life.
- Scan through your life in periods of five years, and list in writing the people who have had the greatest impact on you.
- Scan through your life in periods of five years, and list the people who saw your gifts or who supported or encouraged you to do your best.

Once you have someone in mind, think of a specific experience with that person that captures the essence of the gift you received. Consider these questions:

- What was it about this person that moved you when others did not?
- Did this person enter your life at a time when you especially needed support?
- How did this person's style of being with you help or hinder his or her message to you?
- Was this person aware at the time of the gift he or she had given you?
- Have you passed what this person contributed to you on to others?
- What details do you recall about the person and what you received that make the experience more vivid?
- Are there things this person said or did that particularly impacted your life?

"What is man without the beasts. If all the beasts were gone, men would die from great loneliness of spirit, for whatever happens to the beasts also happens to the man." —Chief Seattle

Animal Friends

*O*ur relationships with animal companions are often among our most important. Whether lifelong family pets or creatures we encounter in the wild, animals are often our teachers and healers. Like the people we know and love, they can bring us important lessons about commitment, love, trust, play, acceptance, and coping with loss. Every animal has a unique personality and way of communicating. Is there a special animal in your life now or was there one in the past? Do you have a memory of a pet from your childhood or more recently?

Once you have thought of a specific animal friend, begin to sift through memories of being with them to start generating story ideas. These questions may help you recall experiences with your special pet:

- How did you meet your animal friend?
- What was your animal friend like when you first brought him or her home?
- What kind of bond did you have?
- What did your animal friend do with their time when you were at home and when you were away?
- What games did she like to play? What funny or playful things did she do?
- What were his nicknames? How did he get them?

- Did your animal friend ever help you or someone else, such as alerting you to an accident or a fire?
- What were her favorite treats, toys, and other animal friends?
- What were some special things you used to do together?
- Did your animal friend ever get lost or separated from you?
- Did he suffer any difficult illness?
- If your animal friend passed away, what was it like when he died?

Your story could be about the whole relationship or a specific experience. If you're writing about the relationship, it's still helpful to include a few anecdotes in your story. You'll probably want to emphasize classic behaviors and rituals that you shared. When you have a particular story in mind, the following questions may help you pinpoint your story's theme:

- Did you learn any special lessons from your animal friend?
- Was there something about him that was particularly lovable?
- Did your animal friend help you when you were going through a particularly difficult time?
- What mattered most about your relationship?
- Did your feelings about him change or evolve?

On the following page is Fritzi Schnel's story about her family's dog, Ziggy. It takes us on a journey of Ziggy's life. Fritzi told us that writing this story allowed her to re-experience in great detail all of her fondest memories of life with Ziggy. "The feelings are now like the photographs, warmly frozen for all time," she said. "If my memory ever fails me, the story has been recorded for my son and future generations."

Our Dog Ziggy by Fritzi S. Schnel

I grew up in an apartment building in the Bronx, New York. Pets were out of the question in my household. My mom was a "neatnik," and even a goldfish was too untidy for her! It wasn't until I was well into my adulthood and living in Northern California that I had the chance to have my own dog. Ziggy was a beautiful golden retriever, the smallest in a litter of nine and born into a family that just wanted to breed their female, no bells and whistles, no "show dog" status. Zackery "Hoover" 4 Jasper, was his official name (as a puppy he sucked up everything in his path, faster than the vacuum cleaner), but to us he was always Ziggy, Zackarooney, Ziggyboy. My tears still fall at the sound of his name. He set the tone for what was to become the greatest friendship I've ever known.

When our son, Danny, was born, Ziggy was already over nine years old. The first thing we did when we walked back into our home was to get down on the rug with the baby and introduce him to Ziggy. We said, "Watch over each other." Our arms encompassed our dog, the firstborn, if you will, but soon Zig took second place to the attention devoted to our child. He was a gentleman; he never acted out, never chewed a shoe or peed on the rug to voice disdain at his loss of position. I know that he felt our love; it never wavered. I would often lay down next to him and touch him and talk to him, and he would put his paw over my arm. It was like we were holding hands, and sometimes I could see his sweet embarrassed look, like we were sharing intimate secrets with each other. I never did ask him where he went the day he took off as a puppy and didn't return until the next day. I prayed so hard. I refused to believe that he wouldn't be back. I can still remember the feeling of overwhelming joy and relief,

hearing the jingles of his dog tags and the thundering sound his paws made as he came charging down the fifty-five steps to our home. He was dirty, muddy, and happy, and had brought two other dogs home with him I'd never seen before. What a friendly guy.

At the age when Danny was ready to play, Ziggy was too old to chase a ball or jump for a Frisbee. He made an excellent fur pillow and allowed many acrobatic leaps over his body —admittedly, with caution and a great deal of stillness. I can still see his eyes following Danny around the room, without ever moving his head. Ziggy made our world a safe place for children with his gentle tolerant ways.

By the time Danny was four, he had to say good-bye to our dog, our family member, my ideal companion, the perfect image of love. One evening, a few months after Ziggy died, Danny added to our dinner grace this phrase that he created from his own heart: "And I am sad that Ziggy died. And even though we can't see him, he will always be in our hearts and all." He says it every night, still. Thank you, sweet wise son, for knowing and expressing the simple truth each day.

It's been over a year now since Ziggy passed on. There is a Sufi saying that goes something like this: "Oh break my heart, oh break it again, so that I may love again." My heart broke into a million jewels of gratitude for having the privilege of sharing over thirteen years with this special being. When we are ready, we fully expect to open our hearts and home to another golden retriever, another animal who will teach us the wisdom of our pets, receive our love joyfully, and create new stories and memories, just waiting to happen.

He had the softest fur and he always smelled so clean, never like a dog. Who was this creature anyway?

"For it was not into my ear you whispered, but into my heart.
It was not my lips you kissed, but my soul." —Judy Garland

Loves of My Life

Love can take us to the heights of ecstasy and the depths of despair. It is through our intimate relationships that we learn our greatest lessons. Love changes us, moves us to take risks, and helps us have compassion for others. Our partners mirror back to us our own issues with intimacy, loss, self-esteem, and trust. Our commitment to remaining open to the feelings that arise when we risk love can bring profound personal and spiritual transformation. Love has many hues—the passion of new romance, the tenderness of a broken heart, the wisdom of mature love. What has been your experience with love?

Think back to your first innocent love and those that have followed. You might want to make a list with a few notes describing what you appreciate about or have learned from each person. What qualities come to mind when you consider each? What words characterize the spirit of each relationship? Go through the questions below about each person on your list or about one person in particular. Perhaps some of the questions will trigger memories that could lead to a story about a romantic partner:

- When did you first meet him or her?
- Do you recall a special time when you were dating, such as the first time you had a meal together at home, held hands, kissed, or went dancing?
- What happened when you first met one another's family and friends?

- When did you first fall in love or know that you were in love?
- Was there a significant moment you shared, such as when you made a commitment to each other or when you made up after an argument?
- Was there a special gift you received from your partner, such as a ring, a handmade object, or flowers?
- Was there a time you felt that your heart broke and you experienced a significant loss?

Often our early love encounters can be a source of vivid stories. Our hearts are open and our senses are heightened as we enter a new relationship. Take a moment to reflect on the early encounters you had with a special romantic partner. It may be helpful to look over old cards and letters, photographs, and gifts to recall special moments and experiences. You might want to include some of these things in your story page. Is there a photograph that reveals the feeling of the relationship? Is there a card or note that speaks to your experience of love?

Each story can have many layers of meaning. With romantic love, feelings can range from the ecstatic to the awful, and this tension can make your story rich. You may want to describe details about the person (appearance, what he or she said, the feelings he or she shared), sensations you felt (your heart beating, warmth, goosebumps, tingling), and the atmosphere (the light, sounds, smells). After you have described your experience a first time, see which details can be added to convey the experience more fully. What adds to your story's gem and what distracts? Another approach is to create your story with your partner. Together you can write the story about how you met or some other gem in your lives, such as when you made a commitment to each other. This approach allows you to include both your voices as narrators, each expressing your own experience.

"We shape our buildings. Then our buildings shape us."
—Winston Churchill

Home Sweet Home

Whether we live in a city, on a farm, or in the suburbs, our home and neighborhood shape our lives. You may feel drawn to creating a story about an important place where you've lived. Here are some questions to help you find the seeds of a story:

- What made this home special?
- Was it a nurturing home?
- Did you have a special spot, room, or getaway place there?
- What are your fondest memories of this home?
- Did you have any adventures there?
- Are there particular times with celebrations or rituals when you feel especially connected to this place?
- How did you come to appreciate it? Was there a moment when you felt it was home?
- If it is part of your past, how and when did you leave it?

This is an opportunity to see your home as a character in your life story because of the powerful relationship that you have with it. Once you have chosen a topic, include details that are relevant to your main theme. Describe sights, sounds, smells, textures, and how you felt there. Was it warm and cozy, bustling and intense? Is it an expression of you and your aesthetics?

On the following page is a story in letter form that Barbara Easterlin wrote to her two children. Barbara describes her connection to a place where their home once was, how that place changed, and her longing to return to it. By writing this story as a letter and directly addressing her children, Barbara makes the experience more intimate.

Dear Emma and Ryder,

I want to tell you about a really special place. It is a small piece of land on a big hill where you can look out and see the ocean. There used to be a house there, with a big wraparound deck where your dad and I would sit in the summer looking out to Tomales Bay and the forest below. It doesn't look so special right now—it's just a burned-out lot on a hillside. But before the fire, it was beautiful. You couldn't see any other houses from inside ours, just an incredible panorama of golden mountains, water, and forest. It was safe and private, and it was the place I had always dreamed about living, even when I was a child.

The view of our land

I grew up in the suburbs of Southern California surrounded by buildings and roads. When I was a kid, I always looked forward to our family camping vacations, where I would get to see forests and rivers and feel nature's rhythms and slower pace. It was there in nature that I found a sense of calm within myself in the midst of a very large, chaotic, and sometimes violent family. I always hoped one day I would live in a place where I could feel that connection to nature all of the time.

When your dad and I lived in our house on the hill, it was easy to come to an inner stillness very soon after arriving home. It was absolutely quiet there, except for the wind and the occasional rustling of a deer outside at night. In the evenings, I used to sit and watch the luminous twilight colors of the big pastel sky as each star in its varying brightness came out of the deepening sky. In the morning, blue jays and squirrels bickered in the pine trees as hummingbirds dove in for their fill of sugar water out of our feeders. It was a place people loved to visit, and we had constant weekend companions. You were conceived there, Emma.

Despite my love for this magnificent place, we decided to keep the house for vacations and moved closer to the city as we began to have a family. Two weeks after we moved, there was a large forest fire. I smelled smoke from the fire even though we lived fifteen miles away. With the first whiff of that smoke, I had a very strong hunch that the home of my dreams was

The treeplanting ceremony

probably going to be gone soon. Three days later when the fire was done burning, we went to see what remained, and it looked very eerie with dank smoke still in the air and the earth blackened. Nothing was left of our home except the foundation and, strangely, some pieces of magazine pages beneath the ashes here and there. It was startling to see how the power of the fire completely overwhelmed everything on the ridge. A few months later, we had a ceremony with some friends and planted a tree.

I miss that place. The quiet . . . the stillness . . . the utter beauty of the thin golden dawn light in the pine needles. The pine trees are about three feet tall now and the driveway is almost inaccessible because of the weeds. With a little time, nature will bring back the magic of the ridge. I would love for you to feel how easy it is to be at peace within yourself when you live so close to wilderness. Even though our lives are full, that empty lot means something to us in our hearts that we hope to return to one day.

Love
mom

"The clearest way into the universe is through a forest wilderness."

—John Muir

Nature's Gifts

O ur relationship to the natural world is often a source of nurturance, inspiration, rejuvenation, and healing. Childhood experiences of nature are oftentimes the most vivid and stay with us for a lifetime. We may remember a colorful sunset, a shooting star, the quiet of a meadow covered in freshly fallen snow, the chill of water in a stream, the feel of a fuzzy caterpillar, the smell of lilacs. Whether in our own backyard or on a trip far away, nature leaves us with memorable experiences that are stories to tell.

To begin, here are some questions to help you find inspiration for a story:

- What special places do you most like to visit? The ocean?
  A forest? The desert?
- What memorable journeys have you taken in the wilderness—
  perhaps hiking, backpacking, boating, or camping?
- Was there a time when you first fell in love with the natural world
  or felt a deep connection with nature?
- Has your relationship with nature changed you?

To help you recall particular places in nature you've experienced, you may want to find a comfortable chair, perhaps by a window. Give yourself a few moments to reflect on places you've visited where there is water, such as a stream, a lake, a pond, or the ocean. Hear the sounds, smell the smells, see the sights in your mind's eye. Take mental notes about any special experiences that come to mind. Then recall places with land, such as a forest, a mountain, a meadow, a desert, or a farmer's open field. See the colors and textures of the land. Now see the sky—the sunshine, the moonlight, the rain, the snow, the stars, and the clouds. Is there a sound or smell that goes with your experience? What feelings arise? Finally, see the animals and plants—the insects, birds, fish, flowers, and shrubs. What experience does their presence bring? What connection do you have with them?

Once you have the beginnings of a story in mind, begin gathering descriptions—colors, sounds, smells, and textures—that evoke this locale. You may also want to describe the trees, water, animals, and other creatures, and how they define the character of the area. We encourage you to include a description of the spirit of the place and how it felt to be there. Reflect on the lessons you've received from the natural world and the impact it has had on your life. What have you appreciated about nature, and what have you received? Who have you become as a result?

On the following page is a life story by Cynthia Schuetz about a week she spent in California's Sierra Nevada Mountains. The background was created by enlarging a photograph on a color copy machine. The contrast feature was turned down to lighten the image. The story text was then printed onto the photocopy.

June Snow in the Sierra

BY CYNTHIA W. SCHUETZ

I was born and grew up in mountains of concrete and steel, a city girl through and through. Now, decades later, mountains of granite and volcanic rock feel more like home. A visit to the Sierra Nevada high country brings me the kind of joy that comes when I feel in communion with the divine.

In spite of my reverence for the Sierra, I used to have a hard time leaving my "Type A" personality behind when we vacationed in the mountains. I would plan just about every minute of my husband's and my visit. I would pour over trail guides, research local restaurants, and bring scads of books to read, mentally calculating how we could get the most from our time. Then during one visit something happened that changed my turbo-charged approach.

My husband, Jim, and I were spending a week in late June at a cabin in the high Sierra, elevation 7200 feet. We were excited that the deep snow had already melted—on our visit the previous June, the snow pack kept us off all but one hiking trail. This year we were sure we would be able to hike our little hearts out.

Hikes carefully planned
Warm June sun, high mountain trails
Snow falls and God laughs.

In the middle of our second night, rain on the tin roof, loud and insistent, awakened me—the first evidence of an unexpected Arctic cold front. By morning there was snow on the ground and it was cold—and we were ill prepared for both. I felt dismayed and even annoyed that the plans I had made had to be scrapped, but felt sure that this winter weather would pass quickly and we could resume our schedule. So many trails, so little time! In the meantime, we decided to go out and see what the world looked like.

We drove into beauty that left me speechless. Big, fat flakes of snow surrounded us. Birch with bright green leaves and wildflowers newly blossomed were white-coated. Wet snow clumped and dropped from pine and cedar branches. The landscape had become unfamiliar. The summer colors of the day before—the many shades of green, the wildflower pink and yellow, the intense blue sky—had been replaced. Now all was white.

We drove off the highway searching for a small lake. We saw no one and heard nothing but a creek abundant with water. Instantly I felt as though I were in one of those old-fashioned Christmas cards depicting a country winter landscape. Jim and I were tiny, indistinguishable figures sketched into an artist's rendering of a scene created by the greatest artist of all.

My disappointment at our demolished plans disappeared. How could I feel anything but joy at this unforeseen gift, at this opportunity to be in the midst of such startling beauty?

Unexpected snow
Covers the June wildflowers
God's gift of surprise.

I became a captive of God's plans, forced to let go of my own. The weather did not clear, the hiking trails were impassable, and for the rest of the week I had no choice but to cut back, slow down, relax. Jim and I read, dozed, talked, played cards, and just stared out at the beauty. And I liked it! I actually found it delicious, my desire to do replaced with delight in just being. I felt in tune with nature's pace—slow and easy.

God offers lessons
Sierra snow in late June
Flexibility.

I no longer take a "to do" list with me to the high country. I now surrender to the pace of nature, which I've discovered means surrendering to the deepest parts of my true being.

"A bird doesn't sing because it has an answer,

it sings because it has a song."

—Maya Angelou

Unforgettable Memories

Unforgettable experiences make powerful stories because they are life-changing experiences filled with strong feelings and vivid images. What are the big experiences of your life? Perhaps it was the day you completed a marathon, when you were in a serious accident, when you traveled for the first time to another country, or when you were present when a loved one died.

Consider the following questions:

- What were the happiest or most uplifting times in your life?
- What were the most stressful or difficult?
- What were the times of great achievement?
- What were experiences of heartache or immense fear?

Sometimes the things we never forget are the results of years of hard work. Other times our most memorable moments happen when we least expect them—when we were touched by the actions of another, had a great idea, or felt ourselves evolve. Sometimes it's obvious, such as in the case of a great loss, why the experience left a profound impression. Other times, it is more difficult for others to understand why something seemingly insignificant has altered your life.

What unforgettable memories stand out amid the many experiences in your life? How were you changed by these experiences? Take some time to recall the details of an experience. For example, if the experience was one of achievement, was there a moment of triumph? How did you prepare? What obstacles did you overcome? Was it worthwhile?

The story that follows captures an unforgettable memory.

When Daddy Died
by Deborah Gouge

The phone woke me up early that morning.

It was my mother telling me that I needed to come home.

Daddy was dying.

My father had been diagnosed with advanced lung cancer about nine months earlier. The doctors had told us he had about six months to live. We took him home, and my mother tended to him as we watched him deteriorate. Before the diagnosis, my father was an active, happy man who coughed too much and complained occasionally of chest pains. Within months, he was an invalid who had lost too much of his weight and most of his coherence as his pain became unbearable.

Those months were the hardest of my life. I had never loved anyone as much as I loved my dad. As a teenager, I was embarrassed by him. He was a coal miner and then a truck driver. No matter how often he washed his hands, his fingernails would never come clean. As I got older, I came to realize that this man who had to quit school in the ninth grade was probably the wisest person I knew. To this day, I don't know how he raised two daughters in the 1950s to believe that we could be and do anything that we set our sights to.

When I reached my father's hospital room, I saw my mother and my sister, Flo, standing next to his bed. I joined them there, at the spot next to his pillow. For an hour or more, my father never spoke and neither did we. He just looked up at the ceiling, his eyes covered with a milky white film. His body rattled every time he took a breath.

Suddenly I realized that I had some things to say to him. And at the same moment, I saw all the reasons not to say them: My mother and sister would get upset if I started talking, he wasn't even conscious so I would upset them for nothing, and on and on. Then I saw so clearly that if I didn't say the things that I had to say, I would spend the rest of my life wishing that I had.

I bent down and began to whisper in his ear. I said, "I have no idea what happens after we die, but I know you don't have to be afraid. Just trust what's next." I could see how scared he was, and I knew it would be easier if he could stop resisting. Dying couldn't be as hard as resisting it was.

Then I said, "I know you're worried about Mommy and Flo." He had always taken care of them. He had done the same for me, but I had a stronger need to be on my own than either of them had. "You don't need to worry. I promise I'll take care of them as well as you have."

Finally, I thanked him. "I'm clear that you've made possible all that I am and all that I have. No one has ever loved me as you have. I love you so much, Daddy." Then I kissed his cheek.

As I stood up, he turned his head and looked me in the eye. I had thought he was unconscious, but my father had understood everything I had said. He held my gaze for a long moment, then turned back to stare at the ceiling. Within a few minutes, his breathing shifted and relaxed. About fifteen minutes later, he died. I knew the moment his spirit was leaving his body.

I felt so complete with my father that I never cried at his wake or his funeral. I had cried so many tears before he left. Now I had no more. At the funeral home, as I looked at his body in the casket, I was clear that that was not my father lying there. My father had left that body for I don't know where, and as he was leaving, I had said my good-byes. The day was January 17, 1980. I remember the date so well.

That was the day that Daddy died and I stopped being afraid of dying.

Heart Openings

*I*n today's fast-paced world, it is all too easy to lose track of what is significant in our lives. What is important can fade into the background as the nagging details of modern life—the ringing telephones, appointments, to-do lists, bills, and commuting—capture our attention. Sometimes we get so overwhelmed that we forget the magic of the moment and the love in our hearts. Then something happens—perhaps an unexpected encounter with a kind grocery clerk—that brings us back to what's most essential. When we take the time to look, we often find that what opens our hearts is the little things, like taking pleasure in the joy of others or seeing the wonder in a child's eyes.

The experience of suffering can also open our hearts. It could be an experience of the suffering of others, such as an interaction with someone who's homeless and hungry or your own personal experience with suffering. If we let in the experience, it will often leave us with more love in our hearts and greater clarity about who we are.

Do you recall a moment when your heart opened? Allow yourself to recall the experience and to be aware of the details. What happened? What thoughts ran through your mind? How did your body feel? What emotions did you feel? How did you perceive others, and how did they seem to perceive you? What did you learn or discover? What was awakening in you when you felt your heart open?

Duane's story, which follows, is an example of an unexpected awakening of the heart. He created the collage by color-copying the photographs and images. He then cut each image out tearing the edges. The final collage was arranged on the copy machine glass with the cross, a three-dimensional object, placed on top for the final copy.

I t was November 1997—winter in the United States but the hot summer in Brazil. I had traveled on business to one of the world's largest cities, São Paolo, and decided to take one day to visit a family in the favelas, massive shantytowns that are home to several million people. I felt apprehensive as we bounced along for a half an hour through a confusing jumble of unpaved streets without names or clear destinations. On either side were small shanty-homes of two stories that had been built by hand with a mixture of fragile bricks and boards. The ground floor of most of these shanties contained a tiny patio separated from the street by bars that ran from ground to ceiling—and it was behind these bars that people lived out much of their lives. It was here that men played cards, children played with their home-made toys, and women talked and worked—with the bars a constant reminder that this was a lawless area into which the police seldom ventured.

Despite the threatening and unfamiliar circumstances, I felt safe when we finally arrived at our destination. Today was Sunday and I was being escorted by a family to visit a church that had been established by Sister Teresina Bosco as a place of refuge for homeless children. In the midst of this lawless and impoverished landscape, this woman of unquenchable enthusiasm had built a small

Soulful Eyes in São Paolo

by Duane Elgin

church—a simple building that could hold several hundred people. We were there to celebrate a dozen young persons in their rite of passage of receiving their first communion.

The church was already bursting with people, so I stood just outside the doorway, sweating in the fiery tropical sun and, occasionally, standing on my tiptoes to see what was happening. Inside stood the perspiring and singing congregation, as four powerful fans mounted on the walls churned the hot, humid equatorial air. Two weathered men played ancient guitars connected to antique amplifiers that could barely be heard above the enthusiastic singing of the crowd.

For the next half hour, I was buoyed by the spirit of family,

music, and ceremony. Then, suddenly, the sea of people in front of me parted and there stood a small figure. It was Sister Bosco who, until moments before, had been presiding in the front. Somehow she had learned of my presence and, without saying a word, she grabbed my hand and began pulling me forcefully through the crowded church. The ocean of singing people again parted as she made her way to the front.

I wondered why she was doing this; I had not asked to be introduced. As she pulled me up onto the low stage, the guitars stopped, the singing ceased, and Sister Bosco turned and spoke to me, her eyes fierce with love for these people. "I don't want you standing in the back where you can't see people," she said. "I want you in the front where you can see their eyes!" Instantly, I understood that it was not for their benefit that I was brought to the front of the church—it was for my own! She wanted me to see that, despite poverty and suffering, here was a community of souls filled with joy, enthusiasm, and love for life. After I was welcomed by hundreds of beaming faces, the singing resumed with full exuberance. I stood at the front for the remainder of the service surrounded by love and celebration. In seeing the spark of soulfulness in so many eyes, I knew with certainty that we are all cousins in the same human family.

Sister Bosco at her church.

São Paolo -- one of the largest cities in the world.

"There are no mistakes, no coincidences. All events are blessings given to us to learn from." —Elisabeth Kübler-Ross

Small Miracles

*O*ur lives are filled with remarkable events and experiences that fill us with wonder at how the universe works. They may show up as amazing coincidences, synchronicity, or unexplainable healing. These miracles usually stand out in our memory because of the gratitude and awe that they inspire in us.

The following questions may assist you in recalling some of the miracles in your life:

- Have you ever had a dream that foretold a future event?
- Have you ever had an intuitive experience of what was happening to someone far away and later found out that it was accurate?
- Have you ever known in advance that something important was going to happen?
- Have your prayers ever been answered in a way that surprised you?
- Have you ever healed in a way that you or your doctors did not think was possible?

If you choose this topic as the basis for a story, place yourself in the experience and describe what happened. Details about your experience give your story immediacy, presence, and impact. What happened objectively in these miraculous moments is open to anyone's interpretation. But what happened to *you* is not. Your experience is the crucial subject to this kind of story.

"To undertake a genuine spiritual path is not to avoid difficulties but to learn the art of making mistakes wakefully, to bring to them the transformative power of our heart." —Jack Kornfield

Moments of Awakening

*A*wakening occurs in different ways: when we have new understanding about who we are in the universe, or when we see that our life is vastly bigger than we ever thought. Sometimes it happens when we feel our connection with the universe in the core of our being as a sense of perfection and peace, or when we know that love is at the foundation of all existence.

The following questions may help you remember some of your own awakenings:

- Have you ever experienced an "aha!" breakthrough that either changed or reaffirmed your spiritual beliefs, philosophy of life, or way of seeing the world?
- Have you ever felt deeply touched by the power of love or faith?
- Have you ever taken bold action on behalf of your beliefs and felt fueled by a force bigger than you?
- Have you ever had a mystical experience, such as a deep sense of inner peace, or a feeling of connection with all that exists or of the life force flowing through you?

Awakenings and spiritual experiences are often difficult to express because they seem so intangible. Given this, if you choose this topic as the theme of a life story, you may want to begin by describing the setting and circumstances of this experience. Then, as you describe it, include descriptions of your feelings, physical sensations, and other senses, such as smells and sounds. As best as you can, take your reader with you on the journey of experiencing your awakening.

On the following page is John Levy's story about an experience that he had in 1947. Given that this happened over fifty years ago, he remembers very little about the particulars. John had to rely on his experience and not on remembered details to tell the story of his powerful awakening and its impact on his life. In the first photograph, John is lying on the floor and, in the second, he is third from the left in the bottom row.

My Life-Changing Experience

BY JOHN LEVY

The most important experience of my adulthood was my introduction to the life of the spirit. I'd grown up without any exposure to religious ideas and had become rather arrogantly disdainful and ignorant of religions and those who practiced them. All of that began to change in 1947 when I was a twenty-five-year-old graduate student at Stanford and attended a three-week residential seminar on the teachings of Jesus, called the Sequoia Seminar. I went to the seminar hoping for a stimulating intellectual experience. Period. Stimulating it was, but also challenging and life-changing in ways that were not at all what I'd bargained for.

The leaders were Harry and Emilia Rathbun; Harry was a very distinguished and popular law professor at Stanford. The seminar was conducted in a Socratic style, the leaders asking questions and inviting us to search for answers. We looked together at various teachings of Jesus and talked about what they might mean for our lives.

About twenty of us, mostly Stanford students, spent hours sitting in groups in intense questioning and sharing, which was exciting and highly educational but also unsettling and challenging. I was struck by encountering so many other seemingly successful and self-confident people who had the same deep uncertainties that I had. Like me, they were unsure about who they were or where they were going; they also worried about what people thought of them.

I resisted all this most valiantly. In my room, I kept an often-replenished bottle of whiskey to allay my anxiety and dull my feelings. The problem was that it was becoming increasingly clear that my life had a purpose beyond what I had assumed, which was to become as successful as I could and to pass my time as enjoyably as possible. What I eventually couldn't deny was that we needed to devote ourselves to discovering what was referred to as the "will of God," and then to committing ourselves to following this "will" to the best of our abilities, forever. Although I was dimly aware that this higher purpose could add great significance and joy to my life, mostly

and, when my parents died, I returned for another seminar. I subsequently left my job and went to work for Sequoia Seminar to help manage the organization and do some teaching. This has led to a variety of jobs in the nonprofit field, mostly in the realms of psychology and spirituality. This has enriched my life in ways I keep realizing and being grateful for—both by giving me a sense of meaning for my life and by enabling me to live in a world of wonderful people.

As I look back on this remarkable shift in my life, I realize how important it is to allow adequate time

it felt like a sacrifice, like giving up my independence and autonomy.

I stayed through to the end of the seminar and left knowing that I would return, that my experience there was some-

for changes to take place—that trying to rush the process doesn't work and may even be counterproductive. I'm glad I was patient, as it is clear now that this provided me with a life filled with a deep sense

thing I couldn't turn my back on permanently. But I also felt that I wasn't ready, and that I needed to stay with my current priorities—finishing graduate school, and then going out in search of status and fortune. I entered the business world for ten years, of meaning and purpose and the privilege of associating with wonderful people. I'm writing this partly as an expression of gratitude to the Rathbuns and the many others who have graced my life in all these years.

6

COLLECTING LIFE STORIES

*The most beautiful music of all
is the music of what happens.*

IRISH PROVERB

This chapter contains suggestions for creating life stories about someone other than yourself, such as honoring a special person, remembering significant events in your child's life, and recording your family history. It also includes suggestions for interviewing other people.

"Family faces are magic mirrors. Looking at people who belong to us,
we see the past, present, and future." —Gail Lumet Buckley

Exploring My Family History

The generations that have come before us are a real part of who we are today. Because your family history is interwoven with the history of the world, exploring the lives of your ancestors may give you new insights into the forces that have influenced you and others. What circumstances shaped the lives of your ancestors? What traditions or values has your family carried on through generations? What are the similarities between your life and the lives of those who came before you? What are the differences?

Family stories are easily lost. With time, the circumstances and details will fade as those who know the stories pass on. So start now by interviewing relatives for stories, recording your own recollections, and perhaps creating a simple family tree that can help generate questions and stories. This topic may seem huge at first glance, but it can be very manageable. Completing even one story or interview about your family history is a rewarding experience, and future generations will treasure these messages from the past.

RECORDING FAMILY STORIES

Reflect for a few minutes on the family stories you are already familiar with—the ones that have been repeated over time. These are the "I remember when" stories that parents and grandparents tell. Take a moment to jot down a story or two that you may recall. It may be one that you have heard many times and know well, or only a snippet of a larger story that you could ask others about to fill in the missing pieces. "Interviewing Family and Friends for Great Stories," on page 116, provides tips for interviewing others.

Below are some questions that may help you discover your family stories. Additional questions can be found in each of the other topic areas in this chapter. You can use these questions to interview family members or to help you recall stories you have heard.

- Where does your family come from? Are there stories about your place of origin?
- Where did your family name come from and has it changed?
- What do you know about where your ancestors grew up and lived?
- Are there stories about your cultural and ethnic heritage?
- Are there colorful stories about ceremonies, rituals, or traditions that have come down through the family?
- Are there memorable stories about family births, deaths, or marriages?
- Are there skeletons in your family closet? What stories would they tell?
- Do you have any unique characters in your family (perhaps someone of notoriety or who led an unusual life)? In what ways were they unique or memorable?
- Are there any stories associated with visiting an ancestor's country of origin? What happened and what was learned?
- What do you know about your ancestors as parents? As people in relationships? As workers?

- What do you know about any special relationships between family members—siblings, cousins, etc.?
- What do you know about the work your ancestors did? What was life like for them?
- Were there any major events that had an impact on their lives?
- How is your day-to-day life today different from their lives as young adults?
- Do you know of any possession that was particularly important to them? Where did it come from and why was it valued?
- Do you know of a particularly joyous time in their lives? A sad time?
- Is there anything that your ancestors have left undone and that you want to complete?
- Do you know if they had any particular hopes and dreams for future generations?

CREATING A FAMILY TREE

Putting together a simple family tree can help you collect family anecdotes. It's also a fun way to engage the older members in your family. A visual representation with information missing can often jog memories. In addition, a family tree provides a convenient way to raise questions about your family's historic events. Fascinating family stories can unfold when you point to a birth, for example, and ask, "What do you remember about this person's early years?" On page 112 is a family tree that includes the canine and feline members of the family.

An elaborate family tree can take enormous time and research, so consider creating one based on only what you already know or can easily find out. Make it simple. If you lack information about your extended family, begin with your immediate family and then broaden the tree to include other significant relatives. At that point, you might want to ask other family members to contribute their recollections.

It might be fun to include one piece of information about each person on the family tree, such as favorite pastimes, occupations, or how each was known in the family. Do your family members have unique traits, characteristics, or skills? Be on the lookout for insightful stories as you do research for your family tree.

There are many resources available for conducting in-depth research on family history and for creating a family tree. The Internet now has several sites that can be helpful. The resources section at the end of this book lists Internet sites where you can obtain tools, software, links, family-tree templates, and databases on genealogy and family trees.

On the following pages is The Carreño Family Tree by Lisa Carreño and a series of short stories that Lisa wrote about her grandmother. Lisa told us that "the gift of writing is the inner click when I pen something that releases a hidden truth. I don't know why I felt moved to write this story as I did. I just knew I'd learn something unforgettable about my nana and myself."

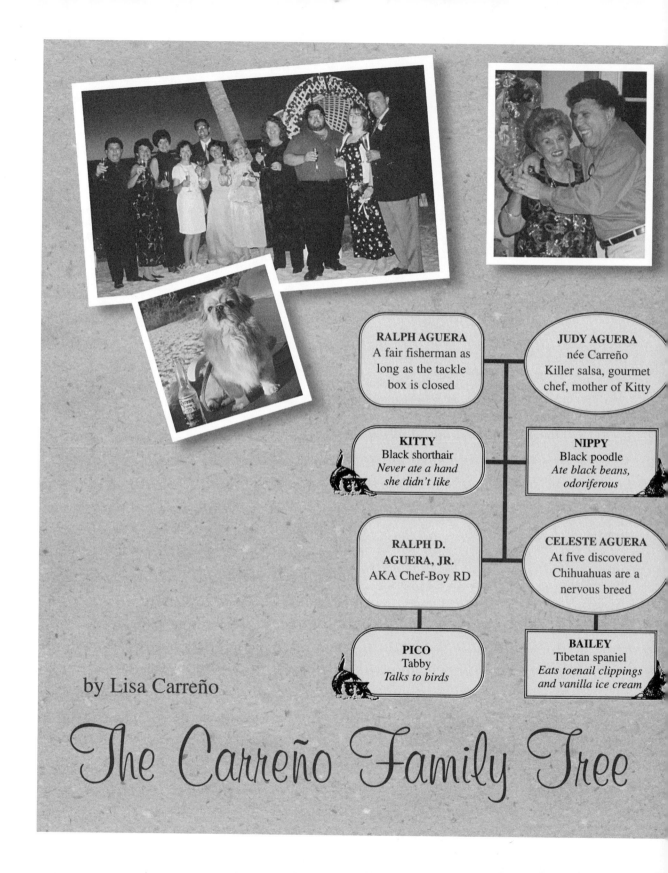

RALPH AGUERA
A fair fisherman as
long as the tackle
box is closed

JUDY AGUERA
née Carreño
Killer salsa, gourmet
chef, mother of Kitty

KITTY
Black shorthair
*Never ate a hand
she didn't like*

NIPPY
Black poodle
*Ate black beans,
odoriferous*

**RALPH D.
AGUERA, JR.**
AKA Chef-Boy RD

CELESTE AGUERA
At five discovered
Chihuahuas are a
nervous breed

PICO
Tabby
Talks to birds

BAILEY
Tibetan spaniel
*Eats toenail clippings
and vanilla ice cream*

by Lisa Carreño

The Carreño Family Tree

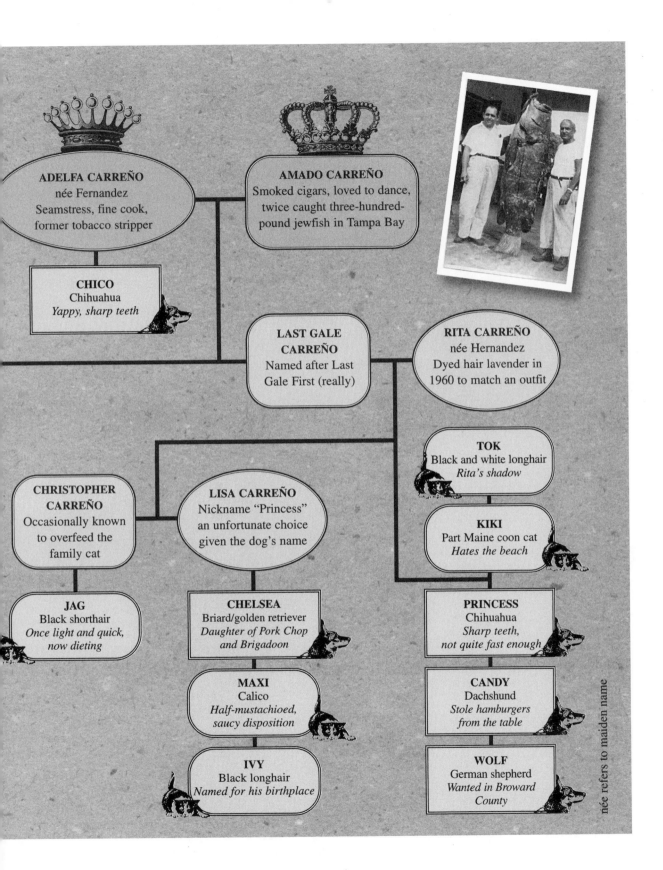

ADELFA CARREÑO
née Fernandez
Seamstress, fine cook,
former tobacco stripper

AMADO CARREÑO
Smoked cigars, loved to dance,
twice caught three-hundred-
pound jewfish in Tampa Bay

CHICO
Chihuahua
Yappy, sharp teeth

**LAST GALE
CARREÑO**
Named after Last
Gale First (really)

RITA CARREÑO
née Hernandez
Dyed hair lavender in
1960 to match an outfit

TOK
Black and white longhair
Rita's shadow

**CHRISTOPHER
CARREÑO**
Occasionally known
to overfeed the
family cat

LISA CARREÑO
Nickname "Princess"
an unfortunate choice
given the dog's name

KIKI
Part Maine coon cat
Hates the beach

JAG
Black shorthair
*Once light and quick,
now dieting*

CHELSEA
Briard/golden retriever
*Daughter of Pork Chop
and Brigadoon*

PRINCESS
Chihuahua
*Sharp teeth,
not quite fast enough*

MAXI
Calico
*Half-mustachioed,
saucy disposition*

CANDY
Dachshund
*Stole hamburgers
from the table*

IVY
Black longhair
Named for his birthplace

WOLF
German shepherd
*Wanted in Broward
County*

née refers to maiden name

Herein Lies Forgiveness

by Lisa G. Carreño

Dear Mother Goddess,

I am awake early. The sky is still gray. I was dreaming I was at Nana's house in the kitchen helping her cook. I was stirring a pot of tomato sauce while Nana cut Cuban bread on the table behind me. Although I was watching the sauce, I could also see Nana at the table. She cut the bread carefully, slowly, almost like a robot. Then she brought the blade down on her left hand, in the soft spot between her thumb and index finger. The wound bled enormously, but she did not stop. She wrapped her hand in a dirty kitchen towel, the blood quickly seeping through the cloth. She came to the stove and with her right hand took the spoon from me and began stirring the pot. I saw the blood coming from her left hand and cried, "Nana, why don't you stop? We need to go to the doctor." Again, like a robot, without ever looking into my eyes, she said, "When I was a little girl, my mother never had time for me."

"Ice water."

Nana's thin, sing-songy voice pronounced *water* with a long "a" sound, about three or four syllables long. What she said came out sounding like *ice waaater*, with an accent on the ice.

The waiter, slightly stooped at the waist to better hear Nana's order but still couldn't understand her. It didn't matter that he resorted to kneeling next to her, cupping his hand to his ear. "Nana," I said, "he doesn't speak English. You need to tell him again in Spanish."

"Ice waaater," she stated again, this time more slowly, a little louder and looking directly into his puzzled face as if a plaintive drawl would better communicate her request.

"Nana," I began to plead, "you speak better Spanish than I do. Why don't you tell him in Spanish?"

"Ice waaater" was all she said. She sat back in her chair with an expression as imperious as that of any queen directing her subjects. It was as though she had never heard me or chose to ignore me. I looked to my aunt and younger cousin, who scanned the *tapas* menu for several selections that would appease all our appetites.

"*Por favor, señor, para ella,*" I pointed to Nana, "*un vaso de agua sin gas con hielo y, por mi, una cerveza Cruzcampo.*" I felt nervous about my Spanish but too exasperated to work out the grammar.

After the waiter left, I looked over to Nana. She watched the people bustling down Sierpes Street. The street was crowded, and other cafés were busy with Spaniards and tourists enjoying the siesta. "Nana, you speak better Spanish than I do. Why don't you order your drink in Spanish? We've been in Spain for five days, and you haven't ordered for yourself once."

She had leaned forward to hear what I was saying. As she leaned back in her chair once again, she simply said, "No, I haven't," and again turned her eyes to the people walking by.

I sighed, looked to my aunt and cousin again, and then searched the café for our waiter and his beverage tray.

My cat Maxi is guarding the door. She is bundled in a calico heap facing me, however, as though she's certain that I need to stay and write until I sort this out.

"Be careful of the Mexicans when you get to California!" Nana once warned to me. I shutter at the memory of why she felt compelled to warn. I am still embarrassed that I did not protest her pronouncement or say something to alter her opinion.

"Are they Cuban?" she asked on another occasion after we'd visited the parents of one of my friends in Tampa. My temper flared but I politely answered, "Yes, why?" "Oh, I was just wondering," she responded dismissively. I didn't explore any further.

"When I was a little girl, my mother never had time for me."

These words ring in my memory as clear as the morning almost ten years ago when I awoke from this dream. My imperious nana, abandoned along with five siblings by her father when she was just five. He fled to Cuba to start another family and never returned. When I think of these words, I can forgive her for just about anything.

"Every story you tell is your own story." —Joseph Campbell

Interviewing Family and Friends for Great Stories

A great way to collect stories is by interviewing family and friends about key experiences in their lives. These stories can be shared at gatherings, distributed to family members, and saved for future generations.

Decide whom you would like to interview and what you would like to know. What gems are waiting to be discovered by asking questions? Do you want to recall and understand life in earlier times? Do you want to focus the interview on one theme, such as adventures in the person's childhood, or do you want to ask a variety of questions to reveal stories from many areas of his or her life?

Most of the topic areas in chapter 5, as well as in "Exploring My Family History" in this chapter, have questions you can use to interview a family member or friend. It may help to have one or two treasured objects available to focus the conversation around, such as an old photograph, a homemade wooden spoon, or a statue brought back from a trip to Asia. A familiar object can be a good starting point for the interview and a trigger for recalling memories.

The easiest way to keep a record of your interview is to tape-record it. Another approach is to take notes and write up the story later. In either case, you may want to give the people you interview a few questions in advance to help awaken their memories. Here are some additional tips:

- Before the interview, check that your tape recorder is working properly and that you have everything you need, including blank cassettes, batteries, and a microphone.
- When tape-recording your interview, speak in a conversational manner, so that the person you are interviewing is relaxed and speaks in a normal voice.
- Give interviewees your full attention. They will feel your interest and respond. Listen fully. If you think of another question while they are talking, make a note and wait to ask it until they are finished talking. Don't interrupt.
- Ask open-ended questions rather than ones that elicit a *yes* or *no* answer. Instead of "Did you enjoy school?" you might ask, "What did you enjoy about learning?" or "What was school like?"
- If you ask a question that they can't or won't answer, don't belabor it. Just move on. Try new questions. Go with the flow. Be open to changing directions and letting go of your agenda. Follow what they are interested in and listen for where they bring more energy to the conversation.
- Ask to see photographs or keepsakes that are relevant to their story.
- Consider taking a photograph of the person you interview so that you will have a visual record of the day of your interview.

Later you can transcribe the whole tape or just what's interesting. Be sure to save the cassette tape as well as the written record. If need be, you can follow up your interview with a few more questions.

"It took me four years to paint like Raphael,
but a lifetime to paint like a child." —Picasso

Remembering a Child's Life

W hether you do it as a parent, relative, or friend, taking the time to record even one story about a child is a precious gift. Later in life, that story will remind the child of his or her childhood tenderness, curiosity, and playfulness. You may want to capture an everyday experience, such as playing with superhero action figures or doing chores, or you might want to focus on a special experience, such as making sand castles at the beach. Here are some suggestions.

RECORD THE STORY OF YOUR CHILD'S BIRTH

If you are a parent, your child's birth is probably one of the most profound moments of your relationship with your child. One day your child will appreciate knowing about that birth experience—the first contractions, the trip to the hospital, labor and delivery, and your first thoughts and impressions on seeing your child. This is a great time to give concrete examples of your experience. If your child is adopted, you may want to create an adoption-day story. You can also create stories about the adoption process, about anticipating and preparing for your child's arrival, and how he or she came to be your child. If you traveled to meet your child, you may want to include photographs, keepsakes from the trip, and notes from your journal. Stacie Jacobs' account of her daughter's birth is on page 122.

Recount First Times

A story about a child's "firsts" can be a precious treasure. The first time he or she took a step, called you by name, rode a bicycle, read, went to school, or made a friend can provide rich content for a life story. Make the story vivid for your child by capturing the little details that make it personal—like how he or she pronounced words, specific things your child said, as well as expressions and body language. You may want to put the story into context by describing what was happening in your life or in the world at the time.

To make it more interesting, you may want to include both your version and your child's version of what happened. It might be the first time you slept under the stars together, when your child fell into a pond and you pulled him or her out, or when he or she was first in a musical recital. After you have written your story, ask the child to tell the story. An older child may be able to write the story with you. If the child is younger, you could tape-record them telling the story and then transcribe the tape.

You can make your story even more intimate by writing it as a letter. By directly addressing the child, it will make your story more personal and it may help you focus on the details that your child will value as he or she grows older.

It is helpful to keep a notepad handy and record what children do and say so that you won't forget. Another approach is to keep a journal of their lives, perhaps writing down significant experiences each day or week.

Interview a Child or Teenager

Kids say the most surprising things. When we ask them about life, we may discover their simple and refreshing wisdom. To interview children or teenagers, you may want to begin by asking some general questions, then see if you can elicit a story about an experience that they had. Here are a few questions that you can use to get started:

- What games do you like to play with your family and friends?
- Tell me about one of your favorite stories. What do you like about it?
- What kinds of animals do you love? What makes them special?
- What was one of the best days you ever had?
- If you could do anything, what would you do?
- If you could visit anywhere, where would you like to visit?
- Tell me about something funny that happened to you.
- What do you want to be when you grow up?
- When you grow up, what do you want to remember about being young?

Have a Child Create a Story

Helping children to create stories can be a fun activity for the whole family. Older children may want assistance in writing their own stories, while younger children may want to tell you stories for you to write out. We encourage you to take word-for-word dictation, as there is something special about children's language. Ask the children to draw a picture or include photographs of themselves, special people in their lives, a favorite animal, or their home or school. Let them know that you will include their story in your book of stories and that people in the future will read it.

For Isabel: The Story of Your Birth

 I stared down at the Scrabble board and flashed your dad a smile. Despite being nine months and two weeks pregnant, I was still feeling competitive. I had been hoping that your dad would put down a word containing a C or G. He complied nicely with "mice." I promptly laid down all my letters to form "crannies." Seven letters—the only way to beat your dad.

A few minutes later on that stormy January night, the contractions started. The first ones made me confident. I thought aloud, "Is this all it is?" Your grandmother Mercedes, laughing, shook her head. "You haven't seen anything yet," she chuckled.

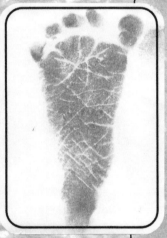

I knew Grandma was right. I had read several childbirth books and convinced myself that I could handle the experience. But inside I wasn't so sure.

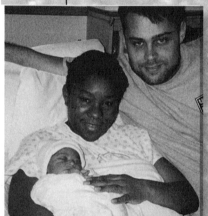

A couple of hours later, a mammoth contraction sent me to the bathroom, sick to my stomach. I made your dad call the hospital. He didn't hang up with good news. We would have to stick it out at home for a while—those pre-meds weren't ready for a potential case of false labor.

As the rain showers outside got worse, the backbreaking contractions picked up frequency until they were buckling me over every seven or eight minutes. At 5:30 A.M., we roused your grandmother, picked up our prepacked duffel bags, and drove to the hospital. After passing the hospital security desk, I walked a very long hallway to the birthing-center elevators.

I spread out my aching body on the delivery-room bed. I received an epidural shot almost immediately, enabling me to rest for two hours. My eyes were closing just

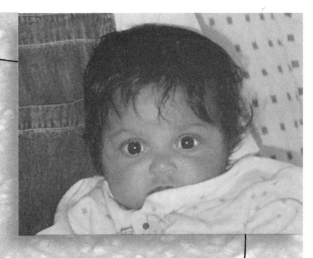

BY STACIE JACOBS

as the city became distinguishable through my room's fifteenth-floor window.

By 11:30 A.M., I was wide awake and ready to push. Your father walked into the room after moving our car and calling friends and relatives eager for the news. His

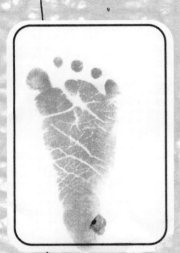

jaw dropped when he heard it was already time for you to make your entrance into the world. After a couple of pushes, the doctors informed me you were "sunny-side up"—meaning you were coming out face up (the wrong way, according to the doctors). They tried to turn you several times. Once you successfully flipped onto your belly but quickly turned back.

Dr. Livingston came in and, eager for you to be born for the sake of your health, tried pulling you out with forceps. When that didn't work, they used vacuum assistance, coupled with all the pushing power I could muster. There was a lot of pulling and tugging. On the fourth tug, you arrived at 1:28 P.M.

You were immediately whisked away to get washed up. I felt relieved to hear your high-pitched cries from across the room. After making sure I was okay, your father nearly ran to the other side of the room, where the doctor was examining you. The pediatrician's smile assured him everything was okay. Your dad brought you—wrapped like a mummy—over to me.

I held you in my arms, and your father and I just cried. They were tears of joy and relief that you had finally arrived. The labor was harder than I had feared, but you were more beautiful and precious than I had ever imagined.

"Call it a clan, call it a network. Call it a tribe, call it a family.
Whatever you call it, whoever you are, you need one." —Jane Howard

Honoring a Special Person

*C*reating a story as a way to honor another person or a relationship can be both a fun project and a wonderful gift for a special occasion—a milestone birthday, a fiftieth wedding anniversary, the day your child goes off to college. Your story can be a celebration of your love and caring, an acknowledgment of the person's unique qualities, or a way of honoring something special you shared together.

In addition to telling your own story, you may want to collect a few stories from other family members or friends. The stories and photographs can be placed in a special birthday or anniversary scrapbook. If they are a memorial for someone who passed away, the stories could be saved for the next generation. If others are not inspired or able to write their own stories, you may want to record them telling a story and then transcribe the tape.

Here are some questions that may help you uncover stories:

- What are the qualities about the person that you most appreciate—honesty, compassion, intelligence, generosity?
- What has this person taught you? What is this person's true gift to the world?
- What is your most vivid memory of this person? How does that experience symbolize his or her life or what he or she means to you?

It may be helpful to recount a particular event and explain how it sums up your experience of this person. Perhaps it shows his or her humor, tenderness, leadership, or playfulness. Recall the details that help celebrate the essence of this person and make his or her life vivid and alive for the reader.

7

ILLUSTRATING YOUR LIFE STORIES

There are always two people in every picture:
the photographer and the viewer.

ANSEL ADAMS

Ours is a visual culture. We use images to advertise, inform, educate, and entertain. Images draw us in. They are usually what engage us first when we see printed material. They are also a key way we remember things. A picture really is worth a thousand words.

Photographs, historical documents, artwork, and other personal artifacts can shape the tone and mood of your story. Your images can introduce the subject, setting, and characters and give relevant information beyond what is in the text. Each image you use has a message, and all the images and text combined together form a whole that can capture the essence of what you are communicating.

There are various ways of incorporating visuals into your story, ranging from the simple addition of a single image to the creation of an elaborate collage. This chapter will guide you through the process of creating an illustrated story. We offer suggestions on techniques that you can use and materials you will need and provide detailed examples of illustrated stories and how they were created. Additional examples of illustrated layouts can be found in chapters 5 and 6.

Seven Steps in Creating an Illustrated Story

Some people develop the story first and then search for photographs. Others do the opposite, starting with photographs and keepsakes as the basis for their story. Regardless of where you start, at some point you will be ready to combine the written text with visuals. When you're at that point, remember that the key is to let the story tell you what images to use. In other words, pay attention to what you see and how you feel as you listen to your story and then communicate that visually.

STEP ONE: DO A PRELIMINARY SEARCH FOR VISUAL MATERIALS

As you write your story, images may or may not come to mind. Whether they do or not, the first thing to do is to gather together a few photographs and other materials that seem to portray your story visually. Do not spend too much time looking, and don't be discouraged if you discover that photos you had in mind do not seem to fit, that you cannot find a certain old memento, or that you're not sure where to begin. You can return to gathering materials later.

STEP TWO: NOTICE THE IMAGES AND FEELINGS THAT THE STORY ELICITS

To help you see and feel the story, answer the following questions:

- What is the gem of the story?
- What feelings does the story elicit? What is the mood or tone?

- What images come to mind as you hear the story?
- Where is the story set?
- Who is the story about?
- Which words of the text call up images as you read or listen to the story?

STEP THREE: GENERATE IDEAS WITH OTHERS FOR COMMUNICATING THE STORY VISUALLY

Think of people who might be interested in hearing your story. Invite them to make a note of whatever images come to mind as you read the story aloud to them. Don't be shy. Think of this step as a brainstorming session that will help you free up your creativity. Take your time. You may want to read it more than once.

After you have read the story, ask your listeners to tell you about their experience. Hold your comments about your story until they finish so as not to influence them. Then ask them to answer the questions in step two. The first three questions are particularly important.

Once your listeners' responses are complete, share your impressions and then, together, brainstorm ways to express the story visually. Use what resonates with your own intuition. If what the listeners saw and felt is very different from what you intended to communicate, you might want to revisit your story. Are you imagining something in the story that is not expressed in the words? Are your listeners doing that? Can you improve the clarity of the writing so that you both experience similar images? On page 145 is a list of ideas that we generated for visually communicating the story "Of Cod and Men."

If you want to do this process alone, review the questions in step two and then read through the story and highlight words that convey images, emotions, and other graphic descriptions. Or tape-record yourself reading the story and then listen to the tape, making note of the images and feelings that come up.

STEP FOUR: CHOOSE A VISUAL THEME

It's now time to sort through the ideas you've generated and decide on a visual theme. The visual theme is what visually holds together the mood or feeling of the story with the other elements, such as the setting, people, action, and the story's gem. The visual theme may be as simple as the story's mood—playful, reflective, serious, reverent, or peaceful. It can emphasize and express the story's gem—your gratitude, something you discovered, or how much you care about some other person, place, or thing. Or the theme can be a combination of these kinds of elements. It is what you want to communicate visually, and it will guide you in deciding what photographs and materials to use and how to lay them out on your story page. When the visuals are done well, the visual theme of the story is communicated to readers from the first moment they glance at the page.

In doing, for example, the visuals for "Of Cod and Men," which begins on page 144, we had to select among several visual possibilities. The main theme of this story is the contrast and the connection between past and present, between the way of life of Fred's dad and the present in which Fred is sitting on an airplane reflecting on his dad and himself. The setting is the airplane and the coast of Newfoundland. The people include Fred and his father. The mood of Fred's story is contemplative or reflective. Given all of this and that we knew that Fred is a history buff, we decided to depict the contrast in the story with a historical visual theme. You can see the illustrated story on page 148.

STEP FIVE: SELECT MATERIALS

Once you've determined a visual theme, the next step is to choose materials that express your theme. Look through the photographs and other materials that you've already collected for your story. Can you use any of these? What else might you use to express the feelings and images associated with your story? There are many different materials that you can use, including photographs, keepsakes, and props.

Photographs are visual reminders of an experience, but they cannot tell what happened, how it felt, and why it mattered. What happened before and after a picture was taken is often more significant than the photograph itself. Combined with your story, however, your photographs can provide context, express a theme or mood, and give additional information that can make the story even more compelling.

When designing your story page, start with photos of the people, place, and action. Include many possibilities at first. Later, as you create a layout, you can set aside most of them. Look for photographs that communicate by showing facial expressions, body language, clothing, actions, home or neighborhood, and background.

Like photographs, keepsakes are connected with the story's history. Keepsakes are items such as letters, postcards, newspaper and magazine clippings, recipes, souvenirs, programs, reviews, journal entries, ticket stubs, drawings, children's handprints and footprints, and documents such as birth, death, and marriage certificates, deeds, and awards.

Props are materials that can serve as symbols or metaphors for the story—perhaps as background on the story page or as frames for photographs. Props can evoke a subtle layer of the story, such as the filmstrip in "Of Cod and Men," which symbolizes the reflection in which Fred is engaged—he is seeing images as if he were watching a film. You might use a leaf to express nature, a child's drawing to evoke playfulness or innocence, a candle flame to represent hope or tranquility, or a nest to symbolize preparations for a new baby. If the setting is relevant to the story, you might illustrate it with floor plans, maps, postcards, or drawings. You can even use color and symbols to evoke feelings and reveal layers of meaning in your story.

Here are some of the things you might consider using as props: sheet music, old calendars, comic strips, maps, stickers, charts, time lines, images from magazines and books, and paper with color, texture, and backgrounds. To add a personal touch, you might use thumb- or handprints, a clipping of hair, drawings, your handwriting, or quotes from your story, books, or poems.

If you do decide to use a keepsake or prop, you can include the original by gluing it onto the page or by creating a pocket with acid-free paper to hold it. (See "The Importance of Acid-Free Materials" on the next page.) If you do not want to use the original, you can use a color copy of the image. To help retain their authentic quality, we recommend that you do not enlarge or reduce keepsakes when you reproduce them; copy them at full size. Photographs, on the other hand, can be reduced without losing their authenticity.

The Importance of Acid-Free Materials

Clippings from newspapers and magazines and other materials that are not acid-free will degrade in time and produce yellow and brown stains. To avoid this damage, it is important that all the materials you use are acid-free. Use acid-free paper, pens, glue, tape, and photo corners. Even many printer ink cartridges are acid-free, such as those made by Hewlett Packard and Epson. To be sure, check with the manufacturer. Acid-free paper now comes in a wide range of colors and textures that can add depth, contrast, and artistry to your page.

Do not use rubber cement, white school glue, or ballpoint pens on photographs; they are not acid-free. You may want to photocopy newspaper clippings and other keepsakes and props onto acid-free paper (using either a color or a black and white copier). The toner in most copiers is acid-free, but it is always best to ask. If photocopying is not an option, then keep these materials on separate pages from your photographs so they are not in direct contact with each other.

If you are concerned about damaging valuable photographs or other objects, you can have them professionally duplicated. Many photography laboratories can do this quickly and inexpensively.

To find acid-free materials, check with scrapbooking and photograph preservation suppliers. Many have Web sites or catalogs. See our list in chapter 9 for suggestions.

STEP SIX: CREATE A LAYOUT

We present two types of layouts in this book: collages and simple text and photo layouts. A collage is a combination of text, photographs, keepsakes, and props that occupies a large portion of the page. By using a number of images, a collage creates a more complex visual story that can emphasize a mood, theme, or context. There are three examples of stories using collage layouts, each of which has a number of elements, beginning on page 148. The three examples also include detailed instructions on how and why we created each particular effect.

Another layout is the simple text and photo layout, which combines the story text with one or two photographs. This method is easy to do, allows for more white space on the page, and is ideal if you want to draw the reader's attention to the subject of a particular photograph. On pages 142 and 143, we show eight variations of simple text and photo layouts that include text, title, and one or two images. There are other examples in chapters 5 and 6.

The type of layout you choose will depend on the number of images you have to work with and the overall feeling that you want to communicate. You may want to emphasize the written text in one story and the visual images in another. We recommend that you try different approaches and discover what works best for you and your particular story.

The number of pages you use to lay out your story will depend on the length of the text and the number of images you use. If your text requires more than one page, consider creating a two-page spread rather than using three pages. The advantage of a two-page spread is that the reader will be able to view the whole story at once.

Whatever number of pages you choose, it's a good idea to create a mock-up of your layout using photocopies of your photographs and other images. This will allow you to crop your visuals and arrange your layout without damaging your originals.

Below are some special considerations for your layout.

BE CREATIVE WITH THE LOOK OF THE TEXT

After you select the type of layout, one of the first things to consider is how you will arrange the text on the page. Design your story layout so that the text style and format do not distract from the written story and its meaning but subtly enhance it. Keeping the font size and style consistent throughout the main body will make the text easier and more inviting to read. However, there may be specific reasons to highlight or vary text size or style, such as when you want to emphasize past versus present voices or the voices of different people. We did this in the story "My Time in Vietnam," beginning on page 154.

Consider using your own handwriting on at least some of the page. Your handwriting is uniquely yours. It's an expression of you that personalizes your story. Those who read your stories in the future will appreciate seeing your handwriting, so consider it for quotes, titles, captions, and even the whole story if you write legibly. Colored pens with different point sizes will create different effects. Try different styles, like print, cursive, and calligraphy. Consider whether to write directly on the scrapbook page or on other paper that you then paste into the scrapbook. To emphasize powerful or interesting statements, you can create a "pull quote" by taking a sentence from your story text and setting it off from the main text body by enlarging it or using a special font. You can also create special quotes or sentences that are not in the main text body, perhaps as a photo caption. See the story, "Our Dog Ziggy", on page 80 for an example of using quotes.

USING A COMPUTER TO HELP DO THE LAYOUT

If you have access to a computer, you can type in your text and format it in a way that will work with the images in the layout. Then you can print it on acid-free paper and cut and paste the text onto your story page. You can also easily produce one- or two-column formats and align your text (to the left or right margins, centered, or justified to both margins) to create different effects. Try out various fonts, point sizes, and styles for the text. Different fonts can evoke different feelings, such as historical, academic, playful, exotic, and avant-garde.

Serif fonts tend to feel more formal and historical. Sans serif fonts tend to be more modern and can mimic handwritten text. Serif fonts have curves or flares on the ends of the letters. Sans serif fonts have no curves or flares on the ends.

Serif **A**   Sans serif **A**

If you have access to a scanner, you can scan your photographs and other images into a word processing program that can download images from a scanner or graphics software package. This will give you the ability to place images as close to the text as you'd like by using text wrap and image placement. More recent programs also have the ability to create text boxes that can be placed inside the body text or in the margins. Many of the simple text and photo layouts on pages 142 and 143 can be achieved with a word processing program with image placement capacities. Advanced computer users may want to scan photographs and use a program with graphic capabilities such as Adobe Photoshop to crop and size photographs. Then you can combine your images with the text and create a layout on-line. If you do not have a color printer, you can go to a copy shop or computer rental center to print your story on a color laser printer.

PAGE BORDERS

You can easily add definition to your story page by creating borders. A simple border can be made along the sides or the top and bottom of the page with a marker using fine to thick points. You can also create a border by repeating small images with a stamp or stickers. See the story "Playing Boat" on page 160, for an example.

DRAWINGS

Your drawings, or those done by a person in the story, may not be professional, but they will make your story page even more personal. Remember that you are not creating a magazine page—you are expressing yourself. Consider drawing symbols, maps, floor plans, and other images that have to do with your story.

Step Seven: Complete Your Illustrated Story

Once you have settled on your page layout, let it sit, preferably for a day or more. If you still like it when you review it again, you are ready to glue down all the pieces (or print it out, if you are using a computer).

It will be helpful, particularly to those who will read your story in years to come, if you sign and date it at the bottom of the page. Dating it will let people know when the story was created. We recommend that you sign it because you're the author and you deserve the credit. Also, if the story is passed on to others, there will be no confusion about who created it.

Suggestions for Working with Photographs

Have you found a photograph that you would like to use but that isn't quite right? Maybe it needs to be larger or smaller, or you'd like to use only a part of it. Perhaps you'd like to emphasize the photo, or explain it. Here are some suggestions for how to make the most effective use of your photographs.

CROPPING PHOTOGRAPHS

As you search for photographs, keep in mind that you can crop out a great deal of a picture. You can use a small piece of a larger photo, or you can enlarge a small photo so that you can emphasize a smaller portion of the whole. You can also emphasize your subject by removing unnecessary or distracting background material. If what you want is the background, you can crop out the subjects in the foreground of the photo. In addition, you can cut your photographs into different shapes, such as the ones in the sample stories at the end of this chapter. If you scan photographs, you can resize them easily with a graphics software program. If you do not have a scanner, you can take your photographs to a photo lab to have them resized or cropped.

FRAMING PHOTOGRAPHS

Creating a frame around a photograph helps set it apart. You can draw a frame using acid-free colored markers or create one with acid-free paper.

It's easy to do. To make a paper frame, first decide on the shape you want for the photograph. Then cut the framing paper in a slightly larger size (so you see a border when the photo is placed on top of it). Transparency paper will allow you to trace the shape of the photographs and frames. The paper you choose for your frame can bring out colors in the photograph.

CREATING CAPTIONS

It may be important to record when a photo was taken and who is in it, particularly when the text does not provide this information. You can hand-write a caption directly onto the story page, or use a computer to type it out, print it on the paper of your choice, and cut and paste it onto the page. You can also write the information on the back of your story page.

WORKING WITH OLD PHOTOGRAPHS

If you include an old photograph on your story page, it may be helpful to find out as much as you can about who and what is in the picture. When was the photograph taken? Why was it taken? Who took it? Who are the people in the picture? What do you know about any of them? What was happening at the time of the photograph? See the story "Remembering Merke" on page 20 for an example of how a photograph can provide valuable information for a story.

Basic Guidelines for Simple Text and Photo Layouts

This is the place for the title

Left:
A 3 x 5 image is integrated into the center of the text body. This creates two narrow columns on either side that contain at least four words per line so that the text can be read with ease.

Right:
The 4 x 6 image, title, and text are centered and balanced in this simple one-column layout.

This is the place for the title

This is the place for the title

Left:
This layout is designed so that the story begins and ends with an image that creates a feeling or atmosphere. Diagonal placement adds contrast and balance.

Right:
Two smaller images are integrated and centered in the text body and can be sequenced to fit the story. The title is centered to bring balance.

This is the place for the title

This is
the place for the
title

Left:
The image is cut into an oval shape and placed in the upper-left quadrant of the page to create contrast in this two-column text layout.

Right:
The diagonal placement of the large image and text block creates an interesting contrast.

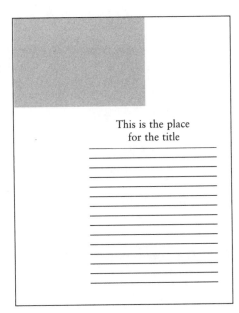

This is the place
for the title

When using three columns of text, center the image and title to balance the page.

This is the
place for the
title

Two small images are placed opposite one another and slightly rotated so that the page does not appear too boxy.

This is the place for
the title

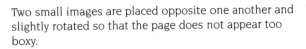

Sample I: A One-Page Collage with a Historical Theme

*T*o give you a feeling for how you can use the seven steps that we describe on pages 128–138, we will take you through the process of finding the visuals for "Of Cod and Men," a story by Coleen's father, Fred LeDrew. We started with the written story. As you read the story below, notice the images and the feelings that the story elicits.

Of Cod and Men

I was flying home to the States after a series of successful business meetings in London. Sitting in first class, at 30,000 feet, being served the best food and wines, I was feeling very content. It was then that the pilot announced that the plane would be traveling down the Newfoundland coast. His voice distracted me from my thoughts and I turned to look out the window. Far below I saw a fishing boat come into view. Plowing through the choppy sea, its dim lights seemed to call out to me. Seeing the white caps and sensing the accompanying chill, I wondered how the fishermen felt. If they could somehow connect with me, would they celebrate the exhilaration of fishing on the open sea? Or would they yearn to trade places, trading their freedom for the physical comforts of my life?

My dad was a fisherman from Cupids, Newfoundland. He often spoke of the cold, wet, and difficult life that came with catching cod for a living. The only insurance a fishing life brought was a roof over your head in a seacoast village and the likelihood of eating fish three meals a day. As I looked down at the fishing boat from 30,000 feet, the contrast between my father's life and my own came together in a single moment when I realized that it could have been me on that boat. At first I wondered if I would have been as successful as a fisherman as I was a businessman. I had reaped the rewards of progress and material wealth, and I was proud of it. Then I wondered whether, despite all the comforts my success provided, if I may have lost something in the bargain. Did I miss out on the adventure of a life at sea with its physical challenges and relationship with nature? As I continued to look out the window, I wondered if these roots of mine are what drives my yearning to fish on that peaceful Maine lake I now call home.

WE DID A PRELIMINARY SEARCH FOR MATERIALS

We asked Fred for pictures of himself and his father as well as any keepsakes that might tie into the story. Fred had only a few photographs of his father and none that connected directly to the story.

WE GENERATED IDEAS

After reviewing the questions, we read the story aloud, noting what we felt and the images that came to mind. Here's a summary of the images and ideas we generated:

- Travel, flying in an airplane
- The coast of Newfoundland
- Fred looking down at the coast from the plane
- A fishing boat in the ocean
- Fish and fishing
- A historical context (a past way of life, Fred's family history)
- The past and present as separate and connected themes

- The contrast between Fred and his dad—between Fred's life as a businessman and his father's life as a fisherman, and between Fred's wealth and relative comfort and his father's difficult and more simple way of life

WE CHOSE A VISUAL THEME

Because the story has a strong link to the past and Fred is a history buff, we chose to create a layout that would be reminiscent of a historical novel.

WE SELECTED MATERIALS

We ended up choosing only two photographs—an old photograph of Fred's father from his wedding day and one of Fred in his business suit. We also chose a number of props: a filmstrip, a picture of a fish taken from an address label, a map of Newfoundland, paper for creating a postage stamp frame, and a picture of an airplane taken from clip art (a digital image).

WE CREATED THE LAYOUT

Since we had a number of elements to use in the story and we wanted to communicate a feeling, we decided to lay out the story page as a collage. To create a historical feeling, we selected a font with serifs that gave a classic feeling to the text. We also included the old picture of Fred's father and printed the story on marble paper that has an antique feeling.

To convey that the past and present are separate yet connected, we did several things. We selected photographs of Fred and his father that were of similar size and orientation and in which each man is in formal attire. To contrast the past and present, we placed Fred's photograph at the top of the page near the title and his father's diagonally across from it at the bottom. Placing images diagonally across from one another provides a more interesting contrast or tension than does placing them directly across from top to bottom or left to right.

To evoke the feeling of looking down at the Newfoundland coastline, we used a map as the background and a picture of a plane taken from clip art to represent Fred's trip down the coast. To create the frame for Fred's picture, we traced a postage stamp making the outline slightly larger than the stamp and then cut out the shape. The photograph was then cropped to fit inside the frame.

To create the impression that the images from the story were like individual frames of a film, we used a filmstrip as a frame and placed each of the images—Fred's father, the fish, and the mini map of Newfoundland—in frames of the filmstrip. Because this story is more about Fred's thoughts than actions, the filmstrip also symbolizes the stream of images that came to Fred. As he was sitting on the plane reflecting, it was as though he was watching a film.

In the end, we were able to bring some sort of visual expression to almost all of the ideas we generated on pages 145–146, except for a fishing boat in the ocean.

Of Cod and Men ~ BY FRED LEDREW

I was flying home to the States after a series of successful business meetings in London. Sitting in first class, at 30,000 feet, being served the best food and wines, I was feeling very content. It was then that the pilot announced that the plane would be traveling down the Newfoundland coast. His voice distracted me from my thoughts, and I turned to look out the window. Far below I saw a fishing boat come into view. Plowing through the choppy sea, its dim lights seemed to call out to me. Seeing the white caps and sensing the accompanying chill, I wondered how the fishermen felt. If they could somehow connect with me, would they celebrate the exhilaration of fishing on the open sea? Or would they yearn to trade places, trading their freedom for the physical comforts of my life?

My dad was a fisherman from Cupids, Newfoundland. He often spoke of the cold, wet, and difficult life that came with catching cod for a living. The only insurance a fishing life brought was a roof over your head in a seacoast village and the likelihood of eating fish three meals a day. As I looked down at the fishing boat from 30,000 feet, the contrast between my father's life and my own came together in a single moment when I realized that it could have been me on that boat. At first I wondered if I would have been as successful as a fisherman as I had been as a businessman. I had reaped the rewards of progress and material wealth, and I was proud of it. Then I wondered whether, despite all the comforts my success provided, if I may have lost something in the bargain. Did I miss out on the adventure of a life at sea with its physical challenges and relationship with nature? As I continued to look out the window, I wondered if these roots of mine are what drives my yearning to fish on that peaceful Maine lake I now call home.

Cupids

Photographs before cropping

Image of a fish taken from an address label

Clip art or drawing of airplane

Color copy of the film strip

Color copy of the map is not shown.

Crop photo to highlight subject. Cut frame in the shape of postage stamp. Layer with contrasting paper.

Use a color copy of a map for background.

For title and text, use font with serif typeface for classic feel.

Print story text on marbled paper and glue onto background.

Paste plane clip art so it overlaps two objects.

Of Cod and Men ~ BY FRED LEDREW

I was flying home to the States after a series of successful business meetings in London. Sitting in first class, at 30,000 feet, being served the best food and wines, I was feeling very content. It was then that the pilot announced that the plane would be traveling down the Newfoundland coast. His voice distracted me from my thoughts, and I turned to look out the window. Far below I saw a fishing boat come into view. Plowing through the choppy sea, its dim lights seemed to call out to me. Seeing the white caps and sensing the accompanying chill, I wondered how the fishermen felt. If they could somehow connect with me, would they celebrate the exhilaration of fishing on the open sea? Or would they yearn to trade places, trading their freedom for the physical comforts of my life?

My dad was a fisherman from Cupids, Newfoundland. He often spoke of the cold, wet, and difficult life that came with catching cod for a living. The only insurance a fishing life brought was a roof over your head in a seacoast village and the likelihood of eating fish three meals a day. As I looked down at the fishing boat from 30,000 feet, the contrast between my father's life and my own came together in a single moment when I realized that it could have been me on that boat. At first I wondered if I would have been as successful as a fisherman as I had been as a businessman. I had reaped the rewards of progress and material wealth, and I was proud of it. Then I wondered whether, despite all the comforts my success provided, if I may have lost something in the bargain. Did I miss out on the adventure of a life at sea with its physical challenges and relationship with nature? As I continued to look out the window, I wondered if these roots of mine are what drives my yearning to fish on that peaceful Maine lake I now call home.

Tools & Supplies

- Computer with printer and word processing program (or typewriter)
- Access to a color copier
- Fine-cutting tool, ruler
- Acid-free pen, tape, glue
- Acid-free paper, plain or marbled texture, variety of colors

Use color copy of film-strip and cut out frames. Place cropped images behind frame.

Sample II: A Collage with Artifacts

*T*he story "My Time in Vietnam" by Pat Tyler pulls together a number of artifacts to create a depiction of Pat's experience while serving as a nurse in Vietnam. There are two parts to the story text: a typed excerpt from her Vietnam journal and an introduction written more recently that creates the context for the journal entry.

Pat had a number of artifacts that she used to illustrate the story, including a photograph from her time as a military nurse, the original journal that she kept in Vietnam, and a collage she made twenty-five years ago. She wanted to include both a portion of her journal and her collage because these were important artifacts that brought character to her story. To retain its authenticity, she reproduced a section of the original journal entry at full size. It would not have seemed as genuine had she reduced it in size. The collage represents a piece of Pat's past and is one of the remaining visual images from her time in Vietnam. It's somewhat chaotic, with rough edges and competing images, many of which are not very clear. Nevertheless, it captures the spirit of Pat's story and is an important artifact.

Next, she had to consider which piece of the text to emphasize. She decided to give emphasis to the journal excerpt because it is the center of the story. She created a box to set off the introduction from the journal excerpt. She chose one photograph to use in the layout even though four were available. The remaining photographs either did not relate directly to the story or were not strong images.

Pat wrote the title so a portion went on top of the photograph, creating a layering effect. Objects can be layered with different papers and by having objects touch and overlap. Layering creates a feeling of depth, connection, and contrast. The thumbprint was added to create a personal touch and to leave a trace of Pat as she completed her story.

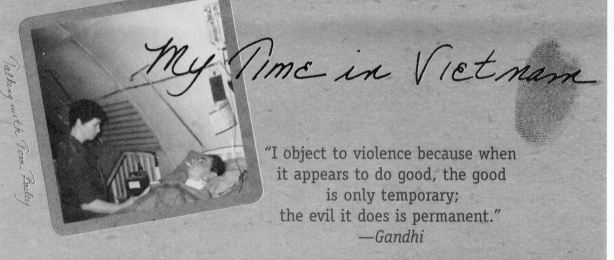

Talking with Tom Bailey

My Time in Vietnam

"I object to violence because when it appears to do good, the good is only temporary; the evil it does is permanent."
—Gandhi

In January 1968, I left my family in Rockville Center Long Island, New York, and flew twenty-two hours to the Republic of Vietnam. I had been an R.N. for one year, and I wanted to be of service in some larger way than being a head nurse of a community hospital surgery unit. A desire to serve rooted inside me when I was ten years old, after I read about Tom Dooley M.D. and how he treated people in need in the remote jungles of Africa. My choices were the Peace Corps or Vietnam. After talking it over with my parents, I chose to go to the jungle of Vietnam. Just before my twenty-sixth birthday on August 13, I wrote the journal excerpt to the right. I had been in Cu Chi, Vietnam, for eight months—an old-timer by army standards. I had answered my question, How could I best use my gifts and serve? My struggle with war was exactly as Gandhi said. If a group of innocent people were being oppressed, how else other than a war would one be able to help stop the suffering? This troubled me for years, and it seemed that war was the only answer, even though it also seemed very wrong.

After directly experiencing bombing, blowing up and destroying people and land, I know that war never was or is or will be the answer to anything. The destruction of bodies and minds and spirits is permanent. It may seem to go away, but it never does. Now, after over thirty years of reflection and writing, I have found that the only way to engage with others and myself under any circumstances is with love and compassion.

A collage I made in 1975

From My Vietnam Journal, August 1968

I'm lying here, listening to familiar noise now. Bombs exploding and machine gun fire. Tonight it seems exceptionally close. It sounds much louder than it does other nights. It may be I'm listening more closely. I close my eyes and wonder what's happening out there. Will they ever come here? Are we as safe as we think? What really goes on in this war when darkness comes? They have hit every area around us now but still stay by our perimeter. Overhead choppers go by. One is just landing. I wonder what has happened. You ask how many ambulatory or litter, G.I. or ARVN. Very impersonal. The chopper flies away only to return later, perhaps.

I'm thinking tonight especially of home. I even cried. I would like to be there now with my family. I won't tell them that because they will only feel sad. It's hard to explain your feelings here. Sometimes you just can't sort them out. You can feel sadness and joy, at one given moment.

Another chopper with more patients. It's like an endless battle. For what? If either side wins, what will they gain? Whatever gains, people suffer; little children without arms and legs, mothers without children, children without parents. A battered people who exist day to day, to feed themselves and have shelter. They know nothing of profit or political gain. They know of hunger, floods, and a life of hard work. The women at 25 look 50. Old before their time because of hardship. What do these people know of anything outside their tiny hamlets? An industrious people with no malice.

— Pat Tyler

Handwritten title connects with journal artifact. Writing on top of photo creates layering and personal touch.

Thumbprint adds personal touch.

Photo framed with colored paper.

Quote was set off with different font size and placed centrally to set a tone.

Collage title includes date when the collage was created. Handwritten title was inverted on color copy machine.

Set off the introduction with a darker frame to create box. Enlarge beginning of the text to create a headline.

My Time in Vietnam

Talking with Tom Dooley

"I object to violence because when it appears to do good, the good is only temporary; the evil it does is permanent."
—*Gandhi*

A collage I made in 1975

In January 1968, I left my family in Rockville Center Long Island, New York, and flew twenty-two hours to the Republic of Vietnam. I had been an R.N. for one year, and I wanted to be of service in some larger way than being a head nurse of a community hospital surgery unit. A desire to serve rooted inside me when I was ten years old, after I read about Tom Dooley M.D. and how he treated people in need in the remote jungles of Africa. My choices were the Peace Corps or Vietnam. After talking it over with my parents, I chose to go to the jungle of Vietnam. Just before my twenty-sixth birthday on August 13, I wrote the journal excerpt to the right. I had been in Cu Chi, Vietnam, for eight months—an old-timer by army standards. I had answered my question, How could I best use my gifts and serve? My struggle with war was exactly as Gandhi said. If a group of innocent people were being oppressed, how else other than a war would one be able to help stop the suffering? This troubled me for years, and it seemed that war was the only answer, even though it also seemed very wrong.

After directly experiencing bombing, blowing up and destroying people and land, I know that war never was or is or will be the answer to anything. The destruction of bodies and minds and spirits is permanent. It may seem to go away, but it never does. Now, after over thirty years of reflection and writing, I have found that the only way to engage with others and myself under any circumstances is with love and compassion.

The type face of the journal excerpt is italic to mimic handwriting. Print text on same textured paper as background paper and glue.

From My Vietnam Journal, August 1968

I'm lying here, listening to familiar noise now. Bombs exploding and machine gun fire. Tonight it seems exceptionally close. It sounds much louder than it does other nights. It may be I'm listening more closely. I close my eyes and wonder what's happening out there. Will they ever come here? Are we as safe as we think? What really goes on in this war when darkness comes? They have hit every area around us now but still stay by our perimeter. Overhead choppers go by. One is just landing. I wonder what has happened. You ask how many ambulatory or litter, G.I. or ARVN. Very impersonal. The chopper flies away only to return later, perhaps.

I'm thinking tonight especially of home. I even cried. I would like to be there now with my family. I won't tell them that because they will only feel sad. It's hard to explain your feelings here. Sometimes you just can't sort them out. You can feel sadness and joy, at one given moment.

Another chopper with more patients. It's like an endless battle. For what? If either side wins, what will they gain? Whatever gains, people suffer; little children without arms and legs, mothers without children, children without parents. A battered people who exist day to day, to feed themselves and have shelter. They know nothing of profit or political gain. They know of hunger, floods, and a life of hard work. The women at 25 look 50. Old before their time because of hardship. What do these people know of anything outside their tiny hamlets? An industrious people with no malice.

— *Pat Tyler*

50

The Journal artifact is a color copy at full size.

Tools & Supplies

- Computer with printer and word processing program (or typewriter)
- Access to a color copier
- Fine-cutting tool, ruler
- Acid-free pen, tape, glue
- Acid-free paper, both textured and plain, a variety of colors
- Ink for thumbprint

Sample III: A Two-Page Collage with a Playful Theme

W hen Coleen set out to illustrate her story, "Playing Boat," she wanted to create a playful story page that evoked the child nature in us all. To achieve this, she did several things. First, she used a crayon to write out the title, inserting photographs of the children inside the letters. Because the story starts with quotes, she used blurb captions to create a comic-book style beginning to the story. In addition, on the first story page, she used drawings created by one of the subjects of the story, her five-year-old niece, Jacqueline. The drawings add a personal touch, and they allow the story to become a mini time capsule preserving Jacqueline's creations.

"Let's play a game!" shouted my five-year-old niece, Jacqueline.

Connor, her brother, two and a half, agreed with an excited smile, his little legs wobbling as he ran around the lumpy lawn of their backyard.

"What shall we play?" I asked.

"Let's play boat," answered Jac.

Boat is one of Jacqueline's favorite make-believe games. Their play set, with a ladder, swing, and slide, is our boat, and the grassy yard around it is the water.

"Get on the ship, everyone," Jacqueline yelled. Connor hesitated for a moment, looked at me for direction, and then we both raced over to our magnificent new boat. We were two ship hands trying to catch the last boat of the day. Jac scurried up first, and then I helped Connor. I sat with my legs dangling off the side, a bit big for the play set. "Get on board!" Jac ordered. Legs dangling would not do. There were dangers in the ocean.

I had begun playing make-believe with my niece when she was just a toddler. At first, I would sometimes feel silly, like a clumsy adult trying to be a child. Then with a little practice, and my niece's enthusiasm, it didn't take long before I began to give myself completely to our play. And what a joy I discovered.

We all looked out to sea. "What's out there?" I asked. "Sharks!" she called out with a ring of excitement and surprise. "Shhharks!" repeated Connor. We all surveyed the waters more intently. Jacqueline spotted a pail at the end of the yard and declared it a baby seal. "We have to save that seal before the sharks get it," she said with determination. We all looked at one another. We knew it was going to be very risky, but we had to try.

With confidence in Jac's leadership, the three of us headed toward the slide. Jac quickly maneuvered down the slide into the water, and I came right behind, guiding Connor into the chilly

waters. On our bellies, we all swam toward the endangered seal, our arms swinging as we stroked our way through the grass-water. Jac scooped up the baby seal in her arms and directed us all back to the boat. "Watch out for the sharks," we all shrieked. We stood up and dashed as fast as we could across the grass and climbed back up to the fort. Pulling in our legs to avoid the sharks and breathing hard, we sat in a circle and smiled at the baby seal we had just rescued. In celebration, Jac fed the orphan some grass. "She'll be okay," Jac tenderly murmured. Connor grunted an "aha." They both gazed at me with a sweet smile. The dark pools in the center of their eyes reflected the sunlight that danced through the walls of the boat. We sat very still, beaming with delight. I knew I was getting a precious glimpse of them, a quiet moment of shared enchantment.

The simple act of playing with my niece and nephew has lifted my spirit. Their imaginations and their delight in play have inspired me and given me hope for our future. My wish to you, Jacqueline and Connor, and to all the children of today and tomorrow, is that whatever life brings, you continue to expand that part of yourselves that is joyous, free, and playful. May your imaginations grow ever wider.

Coleen LeDrew, Dec. 1999

Use a crayon to handwrite the title or have a child create the title and enlarge it on a copy machine if necessary (using your colored story-page paper).

Create white text by using a white or metallic pen.

Create a border with a stamp, marker, stickers, or on a computer.

Print text on colored paper and cut out blurbs.

To fit photo inside letter, use transparent paper to outline the letter, then place it over the photo and cut to size.

Ask a child to draw directly on the story page or have them draw on another piece of the same paper and cut and paste the drawing onto the story page.

"Let's play a game!" shouted my five-year-old niece, Jacqueline.

Connor, her brother, two and a half, agreed with an excited smile, his little legs wobbling as he ran around the lumpy lawn of their backyard.

"What shall we play?" I asked.

"Let's play boat," answered Jac.

Boat is one of Jacqueline's favorite make-believe games. Their play set, with a ladder, swing, and slide, is our boat, and the grassy yard around it is the water.

Enlarge first letter (drop caps) by making space so it fits within paragraph.

"Get on the ship, everyone," Jacqueline yelled. Connor hesitated for a moment, looked at me for direction, and then we both raced over to our magnificent new boat. We were two ship hands trying to catch the last boat of the day. Jac scurried up first, and then I helped Connor. I sat with my legs dangling off the side, a bit big for the play set. "Get on board!" Jac ordered. Legs dangling would not do. There were dangers in the ocean.

I had begun playing make-believe with my niece when she was just a toddler. At first, I would sometimes feel silly, like a clumsy adult trying to be a child. Then with a little practice, and my niece's enthusiasm, it didn't take long before I began to give myself completely to our play. And what a joy I discovered.

waters. On our bellies, we all swam toward the endangered seal, our arms swinging as we stroked our way through the grass-water. Jac scooped up the baby seal in her arms and directed us all back to the boat. "Watch out for the sharks," we all shrieked. We stood up and dashed as fast as we could across the grass and climbed back up to the fort. Pulling in our legs to avoid the sharks and breathing hard, we sat in a circle and smiled at the baby seal we had just rescued. In celebration, Jac fed the orphan some grass. "She'll be okay," Jac tenderly murmured. Connor grunted an "aha." They both gazed at me with a sweet smile. The dark pools in the center of their eyes reflected the sunlight that danced through the walls of the boat. We sat very still, beaming with delight. I knew I was getting a precious glimpse of them, a quiet moment of shared enchantment.

The simple act of playing with my niece and nephew has lifted my spirit. Their imaginations and their delight in play have inspired me and given me hope for our future. My wish to you, Jacqueline and Connor, and to all the children of today and tomorrow, is that whatever life brings, you continue to expand that part of yourselves that is joyous, free, and playful. May your imaginations grow ever wider.

Coleen LeDrew, Dec. 1999

Use two different light-colored papers.

Choose a sans serif font (no flares on the ends of the letters) that looks like handwritten print.

Create photo frames by cutting or tearing paper.

We all looked out to sea. "What's out there?" I asked. "Sharks!" she called out with a ring of excitement and surprise. "Shhharks!" repeated Connor. We all surveyed the waters more intently. Jacqueline spotted a pail at the end of the yard and declared it a baby seal. "We have to save that seal before the sharks get it," she said with determination. We all looked at one another. We knew it was going to be very risky, but we had to try.

With confidence in Jac's leadership, the three of us headed toward the slide. Jac quickly maneuvered down the slide into the water, and I came right behind, guiding Connor into the chilly

Tools & Supplies

- *Computer with printer and word processing program (or typewriter)*
- *Access to a color copier*
- *Fine-cutting tool, ruler*
- *Acid-free pen, tape, glue*
- *Acid-free paper, plain or marbled textured, variety of colors*
- *Crayon, white marker, and transparencies*

8

YOUR LEGACY

Live as if you were to die tomorrow.
Learn as if you were to live forever.

GANDHI

When we record our life stories, we enter a process of self-reflection that often leads to new insights about our lives. As we engage in this process, we may begin to see the patterns that weave through our lives and to discover new meaning in the journey we have made so far. When we see how our stories about the past influence who we are today, we recognize that we are living the stories of tomorrow each moment of each day. In seeing the future already present within ourselves, we may begin to reflect on future generations and what our stories may contribute to them.

As the end of our lives approaches, our legacy to future generations may become more poignant. However, we can explore our legacy at any time in our lives. You might want to take a moment right now to allow yourself to imagine the world after you are gone. Think of those you love and care for and those whom you have touched. As you imagine life in the future without you, think about the legacy you want to leave behind. Think about what you may have wanted to share but have not. For the moment, give yourself to this process. What will you leave behind? What can you do that will allow a piece of you—your truth, your wisdom, what's in your heart—to be passed on?

Questions for Considering Your Legacy

*B*elow are questions whose purpose is not to help you create stories but to help you think about your legacy. If you are a young person, in addition to answering these questions for yourself, you may want to ask them of an elder in your family or community. If you are an elder, you may want to write down your responses to these questions or share them with a friend. Another option is to bring these questions to a gathering of family or friends and record the conversation by taking notes or using a tape recorder.

- What are we most in danger of losing when your generation is gone?
- What important wisdom, knowledge, or experience will your generation leave as its legacy?
- What talents and gifts do you think will blossom in your children, grandchildren, or in future generations?
- What is your biggest hope for your grandchildren and great-grandchildren or future generations? What are your biggest concerns?
- How do you want to be remembered? What do you want to leave for future generations? What can you do now that will be part of your legacy?

A Letter to Future Generations

*E*very story you preserve is a gift to future generations. Now is your chance to speak directly to those friends in the future by reaching beyond this lifetime and envisioning yourself with them. Consider writing a letter to a specific person, such as your grandniece or nephew, or address the letter to all of your future descendants. Your life will be part of their past, and your stories part of the legacy they will inherit. What wisdom do you want to leave for them? What have you learned, seen, or felt that you want future generations to know? Include your signature at the bottom, the date, and perhaps a photograph of yourself. When you have completed the letter, you could paste it onto a page of your storybook, or place it in an envelope and label it "To future generations from (your name)" and then place the unsealed envelope in a pocket of your book.

In closing we would like to offer this affirmation:

May your life stories remind you of the preciousness of this life

and the promise the future holds.

May they open your heart and create kinship with others.

May they be a blessing to you and to everyone they touch.

And may they be a source of healing and wisdom for your soul's journey.

9

RESOURCE GUIDE

Don't be satisfied with stories,
how things have gone with others.
Unfold your own myth.

RUMI

This chapter provides information about different types of scrapbooks, as well as suppliers of acid-free materials. In addition, it includes Internet sites with information on scrapbooking, writing life stories, researching genealogy and family history, and digital storytelling. We also include a recommended reading list.

Types of Scrapbooks

*Y*ou have at least three options for the type of binder or book to use—a three-ring binder, a scrapbook with removable pages, or a bound scrapbook. We recommend that you use a scrapbook with removable pages so that you can work on them outside the book and add and move pages as needed. If you do buy a bound scrapbook, check to be sure that you can lie the book pages flat so you can work on them. Here are the pros and cons of each format.

THREE-RING BINDER

If you choose this type, you will need to get a three-ring binder, 8 1/2 x 11-sheets of card-stock paper, and plastic sheet covers punched with three holes along the side to fit into the binder's rings. All of these supplies should be acid-free. After you have completed working on each sheet, you must insert the paper into a plastic protector sheet, which fits into the binder. Because plastic will retard the natural deterioration of paper, this method provides the best protection for your photographs and other papers. Other advantages are that you can use a variety of paper colors, include keepsakes in the plastic sheet covers, and buy additional supplies—such as a plastic sheet with pockets—that can be added into the binder to hold odd-sized paper or envelopes. The pages lay flat. The disadvantages to using a binder are that the page size is small compared to that of a scrapbook, two-page spreads will have a binder ring in the middle, and there is plastic between the material and the reader.

Scrapbook with Removable Pages

If you choose this type, you will need to obtain an acid-free scrapbook complete with pages. Be sure to use one that allows pages to be easily removed from the binding. Scrapbooks come in various sizes. Many are 10 x 14 or larger. You can take out the pages in unbound books usually by undoing a cord or other fastener. Most scrapbooks do not have plastic sheet covers. Compared to a binder, the advantages of using a scrapbook are that it has a larger page area, and there is no plastic between the reader and the pages. The disadvantages are that the fasteners can become worn if they are undone too often, and you will probably have only one paper color from which to choose. The photographs in particular may deteriorate faster. If you are relatively careful with your book, however, and store it away from heat, moisture, and direct sunlight—preferably in a box or container—it will last for many years.

Bound Scrapbook

If you choose this type, you will need to obtain an acid-free scrapbook. Working on pages inside a book can be challenging, and you will not be able to add, take out, or change the order of pages. It can also be difficult to photocopy or scan completed pages inside the book. Nevertheless, some people prefer a bound book because it keeps all the pages together and makes a permanent book (keeps a historical record of your stories) and is easy to store. As with any scrapbook, it is best to not have pages with photographs facing each other unless you have some acid-free tissue paper or another barrier so the pages will not stick together.

Preserving Your Scrapbook

*H*ow you store your book will also determine its longevity. It is essential to store it in a cool, dry place, away from direct heat, sunlight, and moisture. Here are some other tips:

- Store your book in a box or an airtight container, such as a covered plastic tub.
- Digitize your book by scanning the pages onto a disk for storage.
- Put your digital story on the World Wide Web.

Many stationery and crafts stores carry scrapbooking supplies, including acid-free paper, pens, and glue. Finding the right binder or scrapbook may require using a catalog, as many of the popular scrapbooks sold in stores do not have removable pages.

Distributors of Acid-Free Supplies and Materials

These vendors of archival material will mail catalogs upon request.

Exposures
1-800-222-4947
www.exposuresonline.com

Light Impressions
1-800-828-6216
www.lightimpressionsdirect.com

Family Treasures
1-800-413-2645
www.familytreasures.com

University Products
1-800-628-1912
www.universityproducts.com

Internet Resources

Scrapbook Supplies

These on-line suppliers offer a wide selection of acid-free scrapbooking supplies, including albums and refills, books, computer software, cutting tools, mounting supplies, paper, templates and rulers, and writing supplies.

www.scrapbooksuperstore.com

www.scrapbook-creations.com

www.treasuresforlife.com

www.southernsplash.com

Scrapbook Book and Product Reviews

These sites post reviews of books and supplies (scissors, adhesives, rulers and templates, software, paper, pens, albums, and storage products) by on-line users.

www.scrapbookaddict.com

www.scrapbooking.com

Recording Life Stories

The Association of Personal Historians is "dedicated to helping others preserve their personal histories and life stories." www.personalhistorians.org

Center for Life Stories Preservation is a resource for helping people capture their family and life stories. www.storypreservation.com

Story Circle is a not-for-profit organization made up of women who want to explore their lives and their souls by exploring their personal stories. www.storycircle.org

The Living Legacies Archive at Seeds of Simplicity provides a place for members to share their legacies, a personal life meaning statement or an expression of what is at the essence of a person's life, with others, present and future. Anyone can view the legacies at www.seedsofsimplicity.org

WRITING FAMILY STORIES, FAMILY TREES, AND GENEALOGY

"My History Is America's History" is a millennium project of the National Endowment for the Humanities. Add your favorite family story to a growing collection, search through the stories others have told, create a family tree, and read the on-line guidebook. www.myhistory.org

Family Search Internet Genealogy Service is a collection of genealogical databases created by the Church of Latter-Day Saints. It provides nonsectarian research tools and helps users construct family trees for no charge using surname information. www.familysearch.org

The Genealogy Home Page provides master lists to many on-line resources, including genealogy help and guides, databases, organizations, and search sites. www.genhomepage.com

Ancestor Detective is a self-proclaimed watchdog site that lists Web sites that give inaccurate or misleading genealogical information. Gives alternatives and lists free family tree programs to download. www.ancestordetective.com

Cyndi's List is a master list of over 50,000 genealogy-related links. www.cyndislist.com

ARCHIVAL PRESERVATION

Clarke Historical Library has information designed to help you care for letters, diaries, books, photographs, VCR tapes, scrapbooks, photo albums, other memory books. www.lib.cmich.edu/clarke

New York Institute of Photography offers resources, tips, and on-line courses in photography and digital images. www.nyip.com

Cyndi's List has a category on preserving photographs and documents. www.cyndislist.com

Scraplink has a category entitled "Guidelines for Preserving Your Photographic Heritage." www.scraplink.com

FAMILY WEB SITE

A family Web site can be almost like a virtual scrapbook. These sites offer a free private place for your photographs, stories, calendars, and even chat.

| eCircles | www.ecircles.com | SuperFamily | www.superfamily.com |
| Zing | www.zing.com | MyFamily | www.myfamily.com |

DIGITAL STORYTELLING

Digital storytelling combines not only images and text, but also can include music, voice, video, and animation to create innovative on-line stories that are displayed on a computer screen.

The Center for Digital Storytelling is based at the University of California at Berkeley. It offers stories, activities, a helpful guide, interviews, and links. www.storycenter.org

Bubbe's Back Porch includes stories, links, an interactive Digital Story Bee, and help and suggestions for contributors. www.bubbe.com

Digital Clubhouse Network has facilities in Sunnyvale, California, and New York City. It offers resources, community outreach for people of all walks of life and income levels and projects, links, activities, and stories. www.digiclub.org

Digital Storytelling Conference & Festival, founded by Dana and Denise Atchley, immerses participants in the principles and practice of digital storytelling and provides opportunities to learn from the top instructors and visionaries in the field. www.dstory.com

Recommended Reading

Arrien, Angeles. *Nine Muses: A Mythological Path to Creativity*. Los Angeles: J. P. Tarcher, 2000.

Goldberg, Natalie. *Writing Down the Bones: Freeing the Writer Within*. Boston: Shambhala, 1986.

_____. *Wild Mind: Living the Writer's Life*. New York: Bantam, 1990.

Keen, Sam, and Anne Valley-Fox. *Your Mythic Journey: Finding Meaning in Your Life through Writing and Storytelling*. Los Angeles: J. P. Tarcher, 1989.

Maguire, Jack. *The Power Of Personal Storytelling: Spinning Tales to Connect with Others*. New York: Tarcher/Putnam, 1998.

Moore, Robin. *Awakening the Hidden Storyteller: How to Build a Storytelling Tradition in Your Family*. Boston: Shambhala, 1991.

Remen, Rachel Naomi. *Kitchen Table Wisdom: Stories That Heal*. New York: Riverhead Books, 1996.

Roorbach, Bill. *Writing Life Stories: How to Make Memories into Memoirs, Ideas into Essays, and Life into Literature*. Cincinnati: Story Press, 1998.

Sacred Stories: A Celebration of the Power of Stories to Transform and Heal. Simpkinson, Charles, and Anne Simpkinson, eds. New York: Harper San Francisco, 1993.

The Scrapbooking Guild. *The Simple Art of Scrapbooking*. New York: Dell Publishing, 1998.

Spence, Linda. *Legacy: A Step by Step Guide to Writing Personal History*. Swallow Press/ Ohio University Press: Athens, 1997.

Stone, Richard. *The Healing Art of Storytelling: A Sacred Journey of Personal Discovery*. New York: Hyperion, 1996.

Acknowledgments

$\mathcal{T}$his book grew out of nearly three years of exploration and development. In the fall of 1997, we began developing a book that would guide people in creating a record of their lives at the turn of the millennium. Called *Millennium Memories*, it contained ideas and inspirations for reflecting on the past, life today, and visions of the future. To our disappointment, the publishing world was already filled with books on the millennium theme. So, in 1998, Coleen began the process of transforming that book into something much larger—a book that would inspire and guide people in writing and illustrating their life stories. For nearly two years, Coleen coaxed stories from a widening circle of friends and family and crafted a new structure for this book. Working together with a close community of editors, advisors, and friends, we distilled this rich learning into *Living Legacies*.

Over the three years this book was in development, a number of people made significant contributions to it. Our deep appreciation and gratitude go to each of them.

There were four people in particular whose contributions were invaluable: Barbara Easterlin, Gwen Gordon, Deborah Gouge, and Birgit Wick. Barbara was an early supporter and participant in this project and provided many insightful suggestions. She also gave important ideas for developing the story topic areas. Most of all, she brought her wise spirit and nurturing presence to the completion of the book. Gwen's reflections, sparkling ideas, and playful energy helped move this book through a very challenging final phase of development. She was particularly helpful in shaping the introductory and writing chapters, assisting us in clarifying our message, and providing artistic ideas for the initial illustrated story designs. Deborah brought numerous thoughtful suggestions for the structure and development of this book over the last two years. Her keen eye for editing greatly enhanced its content, simplicity, and organization. We appreciate her steadfast support of this project and its goals. Birgit brought *Living Legacies* to life with her creative and aesthetic design of the book and its cover. She also worked with us on the design of the illustrated stories. She took the many ideas, images, and layouts we had collected and designed innovative and attractive illustrated story pages that would fit the format needed for this book. Her professional and thoughtful approach along with her artistic talents added a great deal to the feel and look of *Living Legacies*.

Justyn LeDrew graciously agreed to test and review many different versions of the manuscript. She provided helpful feedback, unique ideas, and much appreciated encouragement at many points in this book's creation. Pat Tyler has been an enthusiastic supporter from the beginning and kindly shared her powerful stories about her time in Vietnam with us. She helped us in a number of ways, including enrolling her family in testing different versions of the book. Trudy Johnson-Lenz gave us critical feedback at a pivotal point in the book's development. Her insightful questions proved to be a catalyst that helped us to rethink the book's direction. Trudy also provided the inspiration for the opening paragraph. John Levy reviewed the manuscript, provided helpful assistance in a variety of ways, and was a steadfast friend over the years. Robin Brandes brought her talents to early designs for the story pages and continued to support us with her ideas and artistic feedback.

The story creators shared with us the wonderful gift of their stories and patiently supported us with the many details involved in the process of gathering and publishing stories. A biographical sketch for each one is listed on pages 182–184. They are: Lisa Carreño, Barbara Easterlin, Gwen Gordon, Deborah Gouge, Stacie Jacobs,

Elaine LeDrew, Fred LeDrew, John Levy, Fritzi Schnel, Cynthia Schuetz, Elizabeth Share, Genevieve Tyler, and Pat Tyler.

In addition to those already mentioned, a number of people contributed to this book by sharing their stories, testing earlier versions of this book, or reviewing the manuscript. They include Cecile Andrews, Pat and Russel Clough, Christian de la Barra, Bernandatte Dillon, Jacqueline Doyle, Stephen Doyle, Ben Elgin, Matt Elgin, Dave Ellis, Lily Lam, Sandra LeDrew, Denise LeDrew, Vicki Robin and the Systems Sisters, Mary and Tom Thomas, the Tyler family, and Trisha Waldron. A special thank you to Ron Ferris for sharing his story and experience with us. Thank you to Angeles Arrien for writing the foreword for this book.

We also thank the following people who provided assistance or support in different ways: Ralph and Judy Aguera, Margery Cantor, Cliff Elgin, Lynn Gordon, Matthew Holtzman, Peter Johnsen-Lenz, Rachel Naomi Remen, Pamelia Sanders, and Robin Terra.

We are grateful to the people at Conari Press. In particular, we thank Mary Jane Ryan for her encouragement and fine editing of this book, Will Glennon, Ame Mahler Beanland, Leslie Berriman, Heather McArthur, Sharon Donovan, Rosie Levy, Brenda Knight, and Pam Suwinsky for their kind assistance, and Jenny Collins for her cheerful coordination of the production. Thanks to Jean M. Blomquist for her copyediting.

Finally, a heartfelt thank you to Coleen's dad and mom, Fred and Elaine LeDrew, who from the beginning provided invaluable support and assistance that made this book possible. Their unwavering faith and encouragement are truly a gift.

About the Story Creators

Lisa G. Carreño is a weekend writer and full-time nonprofit director in Northern California. She believes she has the best job in the world. The agency's mission is empowering women and children and eliminating racism. Her story, "Herein Lies Forgiveness," is on page 114.

Barbara Easterlin is the mother of two children, Emma and Ryder, as well as a psychologist specializing in relationship therapy. She and her family live in Marin County, California. Her story, "Dear Emma and Ryder," is on page 86.

Gwen Gordon recently left a career in the nonprofit arena to study philosophy, cosmology, and consciousness. She balances her lifelong passion for creating an ecological culture with contemplative practices, creative outbursts, and lots of play. Her story, "Saving Jenny," is on page 74.

Deborah Gouge is a writer and editor who lives in Pittsburgh, Pennsylvania, with her daughters, Laura and Julia. She considers her work to be supporting others to express and realize their visions and dreams. Her story, "When Daddy Died," is on page 94.

Stacie Jacobs is an Internet analyst and brand-new mother to Isabel Elise. Originally from Phoenix, Arizona, she now calls San Francisco home. Her story, "To Isabel: The Story of Your Birth," is on page 122.

Elaine LeDrew is a wife, mother, and grandmother. She balances her time between the East and West Coasts. Her passion is organic vegetable gardening in Maine and her family when she is in California. Her story, "Beach Blush," is on page 68.

Fred LeDrew is the son of immigrants, an avid sport fisherman, and a history buff. Retired, lucky, and thankful, he now spends his time traveling, observing and living his American dream. His story, "Of Cod and Men," is on page 148.

John Levy has followed a number of careers in the corporate and nonprofit worlds. His focus for many years has been spiritual—his own journey and working with people and organizations with that orientation. His story, "My Life-Changing Experience," appears on page 104.

Fritzi S. Schnel has been a massage therapist and healer for over twenty years. Her artistic passion is theatrical and vocal improvisation. She has a cast of characters who focus on humor as a healing salve and teaching tool. Her story, "Our Dog Ziggy," is on page 80.

Cynthia Schuetz recently left her career as a professor to follow her dream of living in the Sierra Nevada foothills. She now is immersed in contemplative prayer and worship, volunteer work, and nature. Gratitude abounds in her life. Her story, "June Snow in the Sierra," is on page 90.

Elizabeth Share is a consultant and nonprofit manager dedicated to strengthening and growing the good works of the nonprofit sector. Elizabeth is the mother of two miraculous boys and the very lucky daughter of wonderful parents. Her story, "Remembering Merke," is on page 20.

Genevieve Tyler's claim to fame is being a mother of six and the grandmother of twelve. She has had a beautiful and happy life and loves living in funky Fairfax, California, with her girls and her dog, Babe. Her life's time line appears on pages 46–49.

Pat Tyler is a wholistic health practitioner and an intern in naturopathic medicine. Pat is a helper and catalyst with deep family connections. Her six-year-old niece, Lacey Helen, says, "You used to be a nurse, now you're a healer." Her story, "My Time in Vietnam," is on page 154.

About the Book Designer

Birgit Wick has always loved to spend hours in bookstores, whether it was back in her home country Germany or now in her new home, the San Francisco Bay Area. To discover beautifully crafted bibliophilic treasures remains an ongoing passion. Her lifelong study of art, design, philosophy, and communication led her into her profession as a graphic designer and expressive arts educator. *When Divas Confess - Opera Singers in Their Leading Roles* was the first book she designed in the United States.

About the Authors

Duane Elgin grew up on a farm in Idaho and is still a farmer at heart. He has a passion for social healing; for example, he has worked for a decade as a community organizer for responsible media. He is the author of three previous books: *Promise Ahead: A Vision of Hope and Action for Humanity's Future*; *Awakening Earth: Exploring the Evolution of Human Culture and Consciousness*; and *Voluntary Simplicity: Toward a Way of Life That is Outwardly Simple, Inwardly Rich*. Duane lives in the San Francisco Bay Area. To find out more about Duane and his books, please visit his web site at: www.awakeningearth.org

As a child, Coleen LeDrew lived in many different places in the United States. She landed in the San Francisco Bay Area as a young adult and fell in love with the natural environment surrounding Mount Tamalpais near where she now lives. Coleen has a background in health education and more recently worked with Duane doing research on indicators of global values change. She is a graduate student exploring and studying transformative learning. *Living Legacies* is her first book.

To Our Readers

Conari Press publishes books on topics ranging from spirituality, personal growth, and relationships to women's issues, parenting, and social issues. Our mission is to publish quality books that will make a difference in people's lives—how we feel about ourselves and how we relate to one another. We value integrity, compassion, and receptivity, both in the books we publish and in the way we do business.

As a member of the community, we sponsor the *Random Acts of Kindness*™ foundation, the guiding force behind *Random Acts of Kindness*™ Week. We donate our damaged books to nonprofit organizations, dedicate a portion of our proceeds from certain books to charitable causes, and continually look for new ways to use natural resources as wisely as possible.

Our readers are our most important resource, and we value your input, suggestions, and ideas about what you would like to see published. Please feel free to contact us, to request our latest book catalog, or to be added to our mailing list.

CONARI PRESS

2550 Ninth Street, Suite 101
Berkeley, California 94710-2551
800-685-9595 • 510-649-7175
fax: 510-649-7190
e-mail: conari@conari.com
http://www.conari.com